Coping with

THE DANGERS OF TATTOOING, BODY PIERCING, AND BRANDING

Beth Wilkinson

THE ROSEN PUBLISHING GROUP, INC./NEW YORK

Published in 1998 by The Rosen Publishing Group, Inc.
29 East 21st Street, New York, NY 10010

First Edition 1998

Cover Photo by Ron Chapple/FPG International

Library of Congress Cataloging-in-Publication Data

Wilkinson, Beth
    Coping with the dangers of tattooing, body piercing, and branding /
Beth Wilkinson.
        p.   cm.
    Includes bibliographical references and index.
    Summary:Gives information needed to make an informed decision
about body modification including the laws and safety regulations surrounding this business.
    ISBN 0-8239-2717-2
    1. Tattooing—Health aspects—Juvenile literature. 2. Body piercing—
Health aspects—Juvenile literature. 3. Branding (Punishment)—Juvenile
literature. [1. Tattooing. 2. Body piercing.] I. Title.
RD119.5.B82W54 1998
617.9'5—dc21   97-45683
                                                              CIP
                                                              AC

Manufactured in the United States of America

About the Author

Beth Wilkinson lives in Laramie, Wyoming. Her major goals are to encourage people to read, parents to read to their children, and through her writing, help young people learn coping skills. Other interests include paper making, candy making, and getting to know people of all ages.

Acknowledgement

A special thanks to my editor, Michele Drohan, who with her excellent ideas and editing skills helped me take this unusual journey into the world of tattooing, body piercing, and branding. With Michele's encouragement I have made lasting friendships with some of the most fascinating young people on this planet.

With respect and appreciation I applaud all those generous people I interviewed.

For KRG
Rosy and Kanie

Contents

Introduction

Body decorating is one of the earliest forms of artistic expression known to humankind. There is evidence from ancient burials and rock carvings to indicate that body art occurred in prehistoric times on the continents of Africa and Asia. Distinctive body painting has long been applied for identification among many peoples and as verification of personal rank or status within a culture. Markings sometimes indicated religious devotion, dedication to magic, or desired protection against evil and disease. For centuries, body and face decorations have been used to enhance the beauty of men and women and have been used to attract the opposite sex.

Native Americans traditionally painted intricate designs on their faces and bodies for many reasons. Often, the painting was used as camouflage against enemies. Sometimes, an intricate stripe or a detailed symbol on one cheek represented the brave deeds done by a warrior. Often, it indicated membership in various religious or political societies or a specific tribe. Painting was even done as protection against the sun and wind. The colors of black, red, and white were made from wood charcoal, powdered copper ore, and clay. These materials were carried in buckskin bags and mixed with bear or buffalo fat before being rubbed on the skin. Most tribes used black to represent death, red for human life, and white for peace. Going into battle, Crow warriors painted their faces half black and half white. Thousands of miles across the Atlantic, Picts, ancient invaders and inhabitants of central and northern Scotland, painted their faces blue for battle.

Face and body painting is still widely practiced in many areas of the world. The same types of plants and herbs used then to make colors and dyes can still be found today. Numerous inhabitants on the continent of Africa use a technique in which the skin is covered with a chalk-and-water mixture and sometimes highlighted by ocher. Often, busy women paint only their faces and breasts, while men devote more time to intricate and extensive body designs of swirls, lines, and curves.

In Eastern countries, kohl, a sulfide powder, is used to blacken eyelids and eyebrows to enhance the beauty of women's eyes. Berber brides of Morocco rub saffron-colored powder into their eyebrows and rouge their cheeks with carmine. Carmine is a red dye created from dried insects. On the women's chins are beard-like tattoos which are considered marks of beauty.

In India, it is traditional with both Hindus and Muslims to decorate a bride's hands and feet with henna. Henna, a natural dye made from a shrub-type tree, has a strong fragrance and feels cool on the skin. The herb leaves are collected, crushed, and made into a powder, then a paste. Using a cone, much like a cake decorating tip, a professional artist creates designs of flowers, leaves, and geometric patterns on the bride's hands, palms, wrists, feet, and ankles. When the artwork dries, the dried paste is rubbed off and the areas washed. The bright orange or reddish designs remain for as long as a month before fading. Guests who attend weddings, banquets, or other festivities may also mark themselves with henna.

Tattooing, a procedure of permanently marking the skin with ink or dye, is not new. In modern Western cultures, tattoos have alternately been regarded as signs of chic and high fashion or as disgusting and crude practices by misfits and sailors. Others see tattoos as a way of identifying with a group or as a way to be different from mainstream culture.

Recently, there has been a surge of interest in tattoos. Large numbers of people from all walks of life are getting tattooed. Young people may be more flamboyant in their choices of design and get multiple tattoos on different surfaces and areas of their body. Older people are usually more restrained in their choices. All in all, tattooing is being experienced by many kinds of people.

For generations, different societies of Africa, South America and the Pacific have practiced ritual piercing of the ears, nose, lips, or genitalia to celebrate the passage from childhood to adulthood. In India, public piercing rituals are conducted on holy days much like they were centuries ago. The body is pierced with wires, long needles, slender knife blades, and hooks. The participants observe such events with parades and feasts.

Currently, body piercing is a hot trend all over the world. Like tattooing, body piercing has taken on new interest among people from all walks of life, especially the younger generation. It is considered on the cutting edge of fashion, and, today, people who work in places from McDonald's to Manhattan's Wall Street have eyebrow, lip, tongue, cheek, and bellybutton piercings.

3

Branding is a raised design on the skin made by searing the skin with an iron. Hot metal sizzles and sears the flesh. In the past, branding was done to mark criminals. This was a common practice in America and England during the seventeenth century.

Today it is sometimes used as a ritual denoting a person's passage from one phase of life to another. It may show a mark of an individual's strength and status or may clarify his or her idea of self-expression and beauty. "A kiss of fire" is a good description of this unusual and radical art expression.

Although branding does not appear to be as popular as tattooing and piercing, the trend is growing. Recently, a magazine, written especially for people interested in body modification, issued a special edition dedicated to the art of branding. In the advertisement section, workshops and classes were offered concerning this unusual and extraordinary practice.

In the '90s, interest in body modification appears to be on the rise. Today, people express all kinds of reasons for being tattooed, pierced, or branded. Explanations may include comfort, encouragement, spiritual and religious need, fascination with art, a generational expression and interest in fashion. If a person is searching for his or her identity, he or she may believe that some form of body art will reflect an attitude and basic position in life.

If you are interested in this phenomenon, you need to know what is involved in getting a tattoo, getting pierced, or being branded. You need to be aware that while it may be the "thing to do," there can be a downside, such as a big investment in time and money, and physical pain and discomfort. Getting a tattoo, a piercing, or a brand on a whim may leave you with a sense of regret or worse, a serious infection. It's important to give considerable thought to the fact that some people have become addicted to body art. You should also understand that tattoo cover-up and removal is not as easy or cheap as is sometimes advertised. Because blood is involved, people with diabetes, hemophilia, and similar diseases should be aware that it is dangerous to be tattooed, pierced, or branded.

It's clear that body art is a popular and modern day trend. And because "everyone's doing it," teens need to be aware what body modification includes. Most of all, they need to know about the risks and dangers before they get tattooed, pierced, or branded. This book will tell you what you need to know to make an informed decision about body modification. It will also tell you about the laws and safety regulations surrounding the businesses of tattooing, body piercing, and branding. If, in the end, you decide you want to express yourself with body art, you will learn all the important information about having it done in a safe, legal, and positive environment. It is hoped that, ultimately, the decisions you make about your body reflect what you really want for yourself and your life.

The Art of
Tattooing

Tattooing is the art of marking the skin with indelible patterns, pictures, or legends by making pricks and inserting colored ink. The word itself has its origins in the South Pacific. The art had been referred to as pricking, scarring, or staining until explorer Captain James Cook encountered the indigenous peoples of Tahiti. In his book *The Voyage in H.M. Bark Endeavor*, Cook wrote, "They stain their bodies by indentings, or pricking the skin with small instruments made of bone, cut into short teeth; which indentings they fill up with dark-blue or black mixture prepared from the smoke of an oily nut. This operation, which is called by the natives 'tatau' leaves an indelible mark on the skin."

The word *tatau* comes from *ta*, which means to strike or to mark in many Polynesian languages. The word tattoo has found its way into most European languages: French - *tattouage*; German - *tattowieren*; Italian - *tatuaggio*; Dutch - *tatoeeren*; Spanish - *tatuaje*.

While the word is a more recent creation, the procedure itself has been around much longer. According to Dr. W. D. Hambly, author of *The History of Tattooing*, it can be traced back to ancient Egypt. Clay dolls, preserved in the Ashmolean Museum in Oxford, England, show tattoo marks on them and represent the earliest evidence of this body art. Dr. Hambly indicates that there is clear proof of tattooing that can be dated in Egypt between 4000 BC and 2000 BC.

Tattooing has been an enduring form of art that has appeared in almost all of the world's cultures. Its many forms represent varied philosophies. In some parts of the globe, it is performed as a religious ceremony or to celebrate a rite of passage, such as when a boy enters manhood or when a girl begins her menstrual cycle. Burmese tattooing has been associated with their religious beliefs for thousands of years. The Ainu of Japan used tattoos to show social status. Tattooing among the Eskimos has its origin in religious and spiritual beliefs as well.

The Crow Indian word "alappaho" means "people with many tattoos." This may be the way that the Arapaho Tribe was given its name. In an earlier century, Arapaho men frequently had three small circles tattooed across their chests. Arapaho women had a single circle tattooed on their forehead. The tattoos on the Arapaho men and women were made by poking the skin with cactus spines. Powdered charcoal was then rubbed into the punctures. When it healed, the tattoo was sky blue.

The art of puncture tattoo reached its most artistic development among the Maori, a Polynesian people of New Zealand. The Polynesians developed their own style of tattoo, called "Moko." Moko includes different patterns that concern certain religious beliefs. The Maori still use Moko during ceremonies and religious practices. Different patterns represent identification in tribal communities and families. They also represent rank or status for men and women.

In Japan, around 1700 AD, the tattoo became a social marking and religious symbol. At the time, only members of the royal family were permitted to wear embroidered clothing. People who were not members of the royal family who wanted to adorn themselves began having large, colorful designs tattooed on their torsos and upper arms. In this way, they could decorate themselves without breaking the law. The Japanese style of tattoo became known for its use of vivid colors and dramatic designs, and remains very popular to this day. The art became known worldwide when it was introduced into Europe by visiting sailors.

Tattooing in the United States

Tattooing also found its way to the United States by way of the sea. Herman Melville wrote about tattooing in his memoirs from time spent aboard a U.S. Navy ship. The first tattoo studio is believed to have started in 1870 by a German immigrant named Martin Hildebrandt. Hildebrandt was a tattoo artist who worked on soldiers from both sides of the Civil War. He opened a studio in New York City, which became very successful.

During this time, all tattoos were done using an instrument with several needles attached to a wooden handle. The tattooer would prick the skin a couple of times per second by hand. Needless to say, it took a long time to finish a tattoo, and a steady hand to do it right. Another artist, named Samuel O'Reilly, revolutionized the art of tattoo when he invented the first electric tattooing machine in 1891. He was also a mechanic and looked

8

to Thomas Edison's engraving machine for ideas. With a few modifications, O'Reilly changed the world of tattooing. In December 1935, *Life Magazine* reported that one out of every ten persons in the United States had been tattooed.

> *After years of a childhood illness Stephanie's doctors discovered a cure. Happy and in recovery, Stephanie decided to celebrate with a tattoo. The tattoo, a serpent and a unicorn, represents her philosophy that if we did not experience sorrow we would never know joy. She feels that having these symbols make them a part of herself physically as well as spiritually. Her tattoo reminds her that she is a survivor.*
>
> *"My tattoos are gallery art. I have mine where I can show them if I want, but they aren't right out in front of everyone. My tattoos are from a positive experience. A new chapter in my life. My tattoos are my badges of life affirmation."*

Tattoos are prevalent in the United States and, it seems, everywhere else in the world. A tattoo can represent religion, politics, history, or a philosophy. It can represent individuality, current chic, or simple whimsy.

"Tattooing has changed," an artist explains. "It's not like the '40s or '50s when a person had to be a brave soul to do anything that was remotely different. During those times, it was daring to have a single tattoo. Today, people are interested in imagination art which is a combination of ideas and concepts in design. They're interested in having statements in the form of art displayed on their bodies."

Tattoo Organizations

To help prevent the spread of diseases, professional organizations for tattoo artists now recommend certain guidelines they say all professional tattooists should follow. Some of these organizations even hold classes for tattooists to teach them cleanliness and sterilization techniques. They say that anyone considering a tattoo should ask the tattooist whether he or she has taken the class and ask to see the certificate of completion.

The Alliance of Professional Tattooists, Inc. (APT) is an organization devoted to the ongoing education of tattooists. Members include tattooers and collectors. The organization offers workshops, which provide up-to-date information on sterilization procedures and complete infection-control guidelines. It also discusses legislation aimed at banning the art of tattoo. Members of this organization are required to use an autoclave, a machine that sterilizes equipment using super-heated steam under high pressure, and have references. After two years of joining the organization, the participant must take a nine-hour seminar in microbiology and disease transmission, which is offered at conferences around the country.

The National Tattoo Association (NTA) is another association for tattoo artists. They limit the membership to 1,000 people, and there is a waiting list. A prospective member is sponsored by an active participant. Application is made by subscribing to the association's newsletter, which features photos, stories, and articles of interest to the tattoo community. Each issue covers a different health-related topic and any recent conventions of interest to readers.

If you are thinking about getting a tattoo, there are several steps you can take to insure your safety. The key word is *investigate*. Don't be afraid to ask questions. Talk to people who have tattoos about where they had their work done. One positive aspect of the tattoo craze is that it is tremendously social and brings people together. The very words, "I see you have a tattoo," guarantee conversation. The more information you have, the easier it is to make the right decision for you.

Will It Hurt?

This is the first question many people ask the tattoo artist. The general answer is, "It won't cause great pain, but it will cause discomfort." But it also depends on a person's pain level. Some believe that women seem to tolerate pain better than men do.

The tattoo artist's canvas, skin, comes in different types. Some artists consider the thin fine skin of a woman to be the easiest and most enjoyable to work on. Thick skin requires more effort to infuse the pigment and possibly takes longer to heal.

However, Karol Griffin, a tattooist with several years of experience, explains, "I don't think skin quality is gender-specific. Skin varies from body part to body part more than it does from person to person. Skin that has been repeatedly tanned is leathery and hard to work with—male or female. I think women are more conscientious about using lotion and moisturizers to keep skin soft and supple, but they may be more inclined to damage and toughen the skin with the sun or tanning booths.

Personally, I found that the easiest skin to work with was that of stocky people, male or female. The skin of heavier men and women is already stretched, and the texture tends to be quite nice to work on."

The Comfort Zone

It's essential to know what the tattooist should and should not be doing before going under the needle. Asking other people who have gotten tattoos about the proper or normal procedure helps a person know what to expect.

A customer should be shown respect by the shop's proprietor and given answers to any and all questions. If an artist should insist that you remove more clothing than you feel you need to, he or she may not be the right artist for you. If you have any doubts, it's important to realize that you can cancel the procedure. Don't go through with it because you might feel bad about wasting the tattoo artist's time. It's your body and you have the right to leave the shop if you change your mind. If the tattooist's attitude clashes with the kind of work you have in mind, tell him or her that you're going to reevaluate your options. It's not worth it to get a permanent marking on your body just so you don't offend the tattoo artist. It's important to speak up and get exactly what you want. If that means *not* getting the tattoo, that's okay too.

"I found one of the artists where I had considered getting a tattoo to be a bit intimidating and controlling in terms of the creative process," says Michele. "He tried to talk me into something I didn't want. He was annoyed not to have complete artistic control. Right then and there, I decided to go somewhere else."

It is also crucial that a person feels comfortable with the atmosphere of the shop where he or she plans to acquire a tattoo. The business should be in a neat and clean studio—not in an apartment, a tent at a circus, a garage, a music festival, or a bike or motorcycle shop. Most towns and cities have more than one tattoo studio. If you are considering a tattoo, you should investigate more than one.

Equipment

Essential equipment in a tattoo shop is the autoclave or pressurized sterilizer which is used to sterilize the tattooing needles and tubes. The needles are attached to a needle bar, which is inserted into a tube and then into the tattoo machine. The needle bar moves up and down inside the tube. Small needles extend from the tip and push ink into the skin. The area where the artist works needs to be immaculate. With permission you may wish to observe the artist at work. For reasons of hygiene, he or she should be wearing surgical gloves.

Flash and Design

Tattoo shops are usually small establishments with walls decorated with flash and the tattooist's artwork. Flash, pictures of the designs for tattoos, come in sets and are drawn by artists. These designs are also available through tattoo and piercing magazine advertisements. A man named

Lew Alberts, a wallpaper designer, is recognized as inventing the first design sheets, known as flash, in the late 1920s or early 1930s.

There are sample books of the tattooist's art on counters and tables. Some books may be filled with the tattooist's drawings and tattoo design ideas. In addition, every tattoo artist displays a portfolio of photographs of the tattoos he or she has done. These photographs clearly show the level of workmanship, including the array of colors and whether or not the lines are clear and straight. Like other artists, tattooists have areas in which they excel. A person looking for a realistic portrait of a relative, or a reproduction of a famous artwork wouldn't choose a tattoo artist whose portfolio consists solely of cartoons, superheroes, and boldly outlined designs filled with random colors. If the studio has more than one working artist, there will be portfolios and pictures of each person's work.

Some people already have in mind a particular design, pattern, or lettering that they wish to have tattooed on their body. Others have done their own art to give to the artist. Either way, the tattooist begins by making a stencil, or tracing of the design. He or she can usually modify any design by enlarging, shrinking, or drawing additions.

Placement

Once a person has decided on a design and who the artist will be, it's time to discuss the placement. Because of his or her experience, the tattooist can be a big help. The artist should know something about anatomy. For example, for work done on the biceps, part of the design could be tattooed in a shallow part of a muscle, making the tattoo appear elongated. If it is placed in a curve that is not anticipated, it may appear out of focus. Also, how it moves with the body can make a difference in appearance. Having the tattoo placed in the exact and proper position is an important decision.

The artist can also help determine the tattoo's placement before the permanent work is done. This can be done by sketching a replica of the design directly on the skin. If a person doesn't like the position, the artist can wash it off and put it elsewhere.

For many people, where the tattoo is placed is just as important as the tattoo itself. This is because having a tattoo in a very visible place on the body makes a different statement than having it in a place where only you or a loved one can see it. Many people who decide to have a tattoo removed do so because it's on a hand or an arm, and it's difficult to hide or cover at all times. When people get older, their lifestyles change, and they may find themselves in settings or situations where having a tattoo is inappropriate. Imagine being invited to your boyfriend's beach house to meet his parents. Depending on how open-minded they are, it may be difficult to make a good first impression with a tattoo on your shoulder. And hiding that tattoo in a bathing suit isn't so easy. Most people don't anticipate all the different types of circumstances they could find themselves in as they go through life. In this way, the decision to get a tattoo and where to get it can be more consequential than you think.

Price

Prices vary depending on the artist. A small tattoo can cost around $45, while a large leg or back piece might be a couple hundred dollars. Prices also vary based on the experience of the artist. The finest tattooers in the nation command between $125 and $250 an hour.

Guidelines for Tattooing

Remember these guidelines before making any final decisions:

- ↪ Visit more than one tattoo shop and take a parent or a friend along for support.

- ↪ Talk to the artist and observe his or her appearance.

- ↪ Ask yourself if the studio reflects your comfort zone.

- ↪ Request references.

- ↪ Speak to clients who got their tattoos or piercings at the shops you visit.

- ↪ Look in the yellow pages of your directory for the telephone number of your local health department. Ask about laws concerning tattoo and piercing shops.

- ↪ Check prices.

- ↪ Learn about the proper or normal procedure concerning the removal of clothing.

- ↪ Look for an APT or NTA decal in the window of the tattoo shop you are considering patronizing.

The Process

Tattoos take time to complete. A small one may take fifteen minutes, another one might take forty five minutes. Some take many sessions to complete. First, an outline is done with an outliner. This is a bar with three to five needles soldered to it. There is also a difference in the pain when the tattoo is being outlined and the tattoo is being filled in. The pain may feel sharper during the outline because the needle stays on the skin for longer stretches of time. The needle stops every minute or so, and the blood is wiped clean. There is a lot of bleeding during the procedure. A shader is used to shade in and color the tattoo. It consists of five to thirteen flat needles or five to seven round needles. By the time the outline is completed, the skin is slightly numb. Some say an outline feels like an incessant cat scratch and shading feels like a continuous sting or an abrasion. But pain is different for everyone. No matter how many people you talk to, you won't know what it feels like until it's happening. It may not be worth the risk for you.

Taking Care of the Tattoo

Getting instructions on how to take care of a tattoo is extremely important. The tattoo artist will give all clients a pamphlet, brochure, or leaflet that has instructions on how to care for a new tattoo. Some of the important instructions will include: wash properly, use antibiotic ointment, and change the bandage daily. A person can develop what is called an oatmeal scab because he or she has not properly cared for the tattoo. Holidays, which

17

mean absence of color, are places on a tattoo where a heavy scab has formed because the skin was not kept moisturized. When the scab falls off, it takes the ink underneath with it, leaving a faded or empty place in the tattoo. The directions will also include the advice not to use alcohol before or after getting tattooed.

Drinking alcohol before getting tattooed is a huge mistake. In addition to weakening your body's ability to deal with physical stress, alcohol thins the blood. If the blood is thinned by alcohol, it will push the tattoo ink out of the skin. While some bleeding is normal, people who have been drinking usually bleed more runny blood that will drip down the skin. For the same reason, it is a mistake to drink right after being tattooed.

An hour before a tattoo appointment, a person should eat something healthy and drink a glass of juice. The body should be strong in order to make the tattoo experience as painless as possible. Some recommend avoiding caffeine.

The stages of healing are: a scab forms; scab falls off; skin is dry; and skin sheds. The skin will be very itchy, but it's important not to scratch or pick at the scab. It will take around two weeks for the tattoo to heal. For a while the area around the tattoo will hurt like a sunburn. The skin will be sore to the touch. If an infection develops the tattooist and a doctor should be called immediately.

Portrait of A Tattoo Artist

Jason has always been involved in art. As a child, he became fascinated with tattoos when he read that Polynesian fishermen tattooed their legs to protect them from sharks. Storm, from the comic series, The X-men, was his first tattoo. Jason drew the design and had an artist do the work. He made the decision to be a tattoo artist when he was twenty-one.

Still in his early twenties, Jason now has his own shop. He does full custom work. This means that, if requested, he can draw anything freehand anywhere on the client's body. "Fine art is expensive," Jason explains, "and it would be easy to spend $35,000 for tattoos on a back piece. Such a work would take six months to two years."

In the beginning, Jason worked for a year as an apprentice and attended as many body modification conventions as possible. He is dedicated and vows that he will always continue to learn about the art of tattoo.

Jason feels that his profession as a tattoo artist and love for comic-book art and movie-making all blend together. He has definite opinions of what is art and what is not. He believes that knowing how to tattoo and wearing tattoos gives a person pride. "I discourage anyone from getting a tattoo on an impulse," he says. "Being cool is not a good enough reason."

This artist is adamant in his philosophy about what is a suitable tattoo and what is not: he will not do tattoos on faces or hands. There are some designs that he will not create for any price. A swastika is off-limits, and he refuses to do any gang or racial tattoos.

"I've known about art all of my life. As a child, drawing came easy, and as I got older, I branched out into other mediums. I remember that my god-mother had a butterfly tattoo on her ankle, so it was my natural desire to learn to do this type of art. At *first, I was going to have one tattoo. Since then, I have sat under the needle for 100 hours. My tattoos now blend together.*

"I believe that it's important for anyone to know what a meaningful step they are taking when they decide on a tattoo. It's important to know what's going on. Basically, tattoos are tribal and represent who you are. I love the art of tattooing. It's my profession and will always be with me. I know skin and how color lies in it. I know the mechanical chemistry of what's happening to my client's skin as I work. People who are tanned or have dark complexions do not show color as well as paler-skinned clients. People with light skin do well with earth tones. A true artist will 'place colors.' Someone who is not trained or is a bad tattooist is called a 'scratcher.' Their work is uneven and discolored. Anyone like this is disrespectful to the art and heritage of the serious tattoo artist. The equipment for sterilizing material is important. Someone that doesn't use an autoclave is not professional and certainly doesn't care about a client."

Be on the Safe Side

Undergoing the procedure of tattoo is hazardous for anyone with serious health problems, such as diabetes or anemia. People with hemophilia or any other blood disease should not get tattoos because they cannot afford even small losses of blood. It's also important to get the advice and consent of a doctor if you are taking medication. Pregnancy is not a barrier to being tattooed but to be on the safe side, contact the family doctor.

AIDS (acquired immune deficiency syndrome) is caused by the human immunodeficiency virus (HIV). HIV is spread through body fluids, such as blood and semen. People become infected with HIV by having unsafe sex or by sharing an injection needle with someone who is already infected with HIV. People who are at risk can include those who get tattoos or body piercings done at places where equipment is not properly cleaned.

At this time, there have been no reports of anyone contracting AIDS from being tattooed, pierced, or branded in a professional shop. The prolonged incubation period of AIDS makes documentation of the disease, transmitted by tattoo or piercing, difficult. Extreme caution is necessary when having any of these procedures done because there is contact with blood. This is a very important reason to be tattooed in a sterile and professional environment.

Other Health Risks

As the popularity of tattoos continues to rise, concerns about infections also continue to rise. In 1996, the American Medical Association (AMA) stated: "The application of tattoos may present a risk of acquiring bacterial and viral infections, and other complications including allergic reactions to the dyes." Many dermatologists have reported diagnosing boils, the herpes simplex virus, and hepatitis, a dangerous liver disease, develop as a result of unclean equipment.

In an unusual case in Toronto, Ontario, a young woman was admitted to the hospital for back pain and doctors ordered magnetic resonance imaging (MRI). The patient lies down in a tunnel-like machine, and an MRI takes pictures of the body's insides using a magnetic field. The young woman cried out in pain when the procedure started, pointing to her small, flower tattoo. The doctor did some investigating and found that the dyes in that tattoo contained iron oxide. The iron oxide can cause problems with an MRI because it's a magnetic metal. The iron oxide converted the MRI pulses into electricity, causing the young woman to feel an electric current, or shock. Before she could go back to the doctor, she had to have her tattoo removed.

Rite of Passage?

In early times, cave drawings and petroglyphs served the dual purpose of storytelling and recording the day-to-day description of early human's lives. Body tattoos served the same purpose: to mark a time or rite of passage. In our society today, there are few ceremonies to mark the passage from puberty to manhood or womanhood. In Catholic religion, there is confirmation. In Jewish religion, there is a bar or bat mitzvah. In the past as well as today, a tattoo marks the arrival of adulthood for many youths.

In her book, *Coming of Age in Samoa*, Margaret Mead states that "formally the adolescent boy faced tattooing, a painful wearisome proceeding, additionally stressed by group ceremony and taboo." Mead writes that today, tattooing is performed at a much more advanced age and has no connection with puberty; the ceremonies have vanished and it has become a mere matter of a fee to the artist.

22

Times, just as people, change. With modern equipment the process of getting a tattoo has been simplified. Today, tattooing is a matter of trend, style, and peer pressure. A fact of life is that people grow older. What was cool at age fifteen might not be so fantastic at fifty. Deciding to get a tattoo requires some major consideration. Tattoo artist Jonathan I. Shaw, who has been practicing for over twenty years says, "When people are young and following trends and reading *Details Magazine* and watching MTV, they tend to make bad decisions. I see a lot of people getting tattoos who are going to regret it." Remember, it is a decision that you have to live with for the rest of your life.

Body Piercing

Like tattooing, body piercing is sweeping the country. No parts of the body are exempt. Perhaps the saying, "Beauty is in the eye of the beholder," should be changed to "Beauty is in the eyebrow of the beholder." Besides eyebrows, belly button piercings are "in." Piercings for the lip, tongue, and nose are high on the trend list, and multiple piercings for ears are hot. Nothing is off-limits. These days, everything is being pierced on the body, including genitals and nipples. Forehead piercing is done less because there is less skin on that area of the face, which makes it more difficult. Even piercing earlobes is considered minor surgery.

"There isn't as much negative response today to piercing as there was to tattoos twenty years ago," says tattoo artist Salome. "Back then, biker trash and drunken sailors got tattooed, and piercing was the cultural practice of obscure African and South American peoples. Now, piercing is a fashion that is more popular among younger people than older people. However, people who would have been threatened and disapproving back then are getting used to it. Lots of individuals, from different segments of society, CEOs, Wall Street professionals, doctors, and lawyers, are getting piercings."

Body piercing, the cousin of tattooing, has been around for a long time. It can be traced back to Rome 400 to 200

AD. The Romans pierced a metal ring through the foreskin (a fold of skin that covers the glans of the penis) of slaves and athletes. The purpose was to prevent erections so that athletes would perform better. It was believed that any sexual activity would take away energy needed for athletic performance. Slaves were supposedly pierced because they were forbidden to reproduce.

When first encountered by the French, a tribe of Native Americans was given the name of Nez Perce because members of the tribe wore pendants attached to their pierced noses. In today's world, nose rings are common ornaments among the peoples of New Guinea, Africa, Indonesia, Australia, and North and South America. Jewelry that embellishes piercings is usually a symbol of status. In India, it is a sign of beauty for women to have their noses pierced.

Many people living on the continent of Africa pierce the upper portion of their ears. Then, for decorative purpose, the men, women, or children insert copper loops of wire. Some adults also wear earlobe plugs as part of everyday adornment. To do this, a pierce is made in the lobes of the ears, and, over a period of time, increasingly larger plates or cylinders of clay, metal, or wood are inserted until the fatty tissue stretches.

Prince Albert (1819-1861), Queen Victoria's husband, is probably better known for his piercing than as a member of the royal family. A "Prince Albert" is a piercing through the urethra which is located at the base of the penis head. Here, a ring is attached. This adornment was called a "dressing ring" by nineteenth-century tailors. It is believed that Albert wore such a ring to secure his genitalia in either the left or right pant leg of the tight-legged trousers that were the fashion at the time.

Molly is a college student and has a summer job in Cortez, Colorado. The shop where she works specializes in Navajo rugs, silver and turquoise jewelry, intricate bead work, and rare pottery. Molly likes working here because the merchandise she sells is intriguing and beautiful. She enjoys things that are different.

Molly has three ear piercings in her right ear and four ear piercings in her left ear. She also has a piercing in the lower center of her lip. She had this done in a piercing shop. When she's not at work, she wears a silver lip ring. It is decorated with a hematite bead.

Molly's birthplace is Addis Ababa in the country of Ethiopia. Over the years Molly has visited there many times and has always been fascinated with the people in a small mountainous area called Surma. Little is known about the small, isolated group of people, even by anthropologists. Molly had her lower lip pierced as a tribute to this culture, which practices lip piercing.

In her late teens a Surma woman's lower lip is pierced, a painful process that can lead to infection. A small disk is inserted and gradually replaced by larger clay plates over the course of a year. It is believed that the larger the lip plate the more beautiful the bride. The size determines the number of cattle asked by a bride's parents for her hand in marriage. Without the plate, the lower lip is a loop of hanging skin.

Ear Piercing

To pierce her ears, the pioneer girl developed a simple technique. Placing a small potato behind her ear, she quickly ran a hot needle through the lobe. A slim piece of straw was then pulled through the hole and left until healed. Most women wore small gold hoops. A fortunate few were able to afford something more ornate, perhaps even decorated with a pearl or tiny diamond.

During the 1940s, pierced ears and small earrings were considered out-of-fashion. Large clip-ons or heavy hoops and chunky earrings became the style. After a few years, the fashion once again changed, and the trend for tiny and delicate earrings returned. Most often, piercing was done in the home. Eventually, beauty shops, jewelry stores, and discount houses offered ear piercing as a service. Reasonably priced gemstone earrings became available and were a popular jewelry of the 1970s. During the 1980s both men and women started acquiring multiple piercings sweeping upward into the ear cartilages. Today, it is common for both women and men to have their ear's pierced.

While ear piercing is a common and accepted practice, it can still cause serious complications. It is wise for anyone to have his or her ears pierced by a health professional. Sterile conditions and proper placement of the punctures are important.

Piercing can be done with a sterile needle or with a piercing gun, a device that punctures the earlobe while inserting the sterilized post of the earring. Self-piercing with sewing needles or other instruments can lead to infection and should be avoided.

Newspaper Headline: Infection Nearly Takes Girl's Pierced Ear

Recently, an article in the Denver Post *reported that a twelve-year-old girl named Jenna almost lost an ear because of infection. The young girl is recovering from surgery after her ear swelled to twice its normal size, throbbing with pain.*

Her doctor, James M. Jaskunas, a pediatric ear, nose, and throat physician, said, "This is by far the worst infection that I've ever seen." People need to remember that there is a risk in piercing various body parts. It is a surgical procedure. "There was a possibility that Jenna could have lost the ear, or had it seriously deformed," the physician said.

Jenna's problems began when she caught a silver stud earring on a blanket, tearing the cartilage in the upper portion of her ear, where it had been pierced at a shop in a mall. About a week after she tore it, her entire ear became swollen and inflamed. "My ear had turned purple and my head throbbed," Jenny said. "I was scared." She sought medical attention from her family doctor. When oral antibiotics failed to improve her condition, Jenna was referred to Dr. Jaskunas, who ordered her into surgery immediately. In the operating room, doctors drained the infection from Jenna's ear.

Later, they took cultures from the infected area and discovered that the young girl had contracted a virulent bacteria that could only be battled with antibiotics administered intravenously three times a day by private nurses.

"The cultures showed a powerful, resistant bacteria,"

said the doctor. "But with the IV antibiotics, we saw nearly immediate improvement."

Profile of a Piercer

Karol is a tattoo artist. She apprenticed under a well-known tattooist named Slade. She also learned how to pierce. When Karol invested in her own business, she decided to offer piercing services because she observed that tattooed people are interested in piercing and vice versa. Karol also explains that many tattoo shops offer piercing because much of the needed equipment to pierce, the autoclave for instance, is already available in the shop.

Virtually any part of the body can be pierced, and piercing is much more complicated than one might imagine. Anyone thinking about body piercing should seek a professional piercer who has a thorough knowledge of muscle and nerve structure as well as an eye for symmetry. A sense of empathy and compassion for the process of piercing are also necessary.

Bizarre as it sounds, some people enjoy inflicting pain on others, and being paid to do this makes piercing an attractive occupation. Fortunately, these people do not last long in a professional piercing shop. In addition to lacking a sense of concern, they usually become sloppy about the technical aspects of the process and turn out inferior work. It doesn't take long for this sort of information to get around, and ultimately the business fails.

Today, the people who find careers in piercing often refer to it as primitive art. Influential artists publish magazines, speak at piercing seminars, and share piercings and techniques that they have perfected. At these meetings, they cover information about legal and ethical business practices.

An apprentice often becomes involved in a demanding training course under the supervision of a master piercer who may charge a tuition fee of several thousand dollars. It is paramount for the student to learn about cleanliness, disinfectants, chemicals, and supplies. Knowledge is necessary about testing the autoclave to ensure that it is free from contamination. The piercer must also learn how to deal with aftercare and any complications.

Another important skill for a beginner to acquire is a sharp eye. Knowing the best placement for piercings and the appropriate jewelry gauge, size, and color is basic. Sometimes, a novice can learn further information about piercing in massage schools or community college anatomy and physiology courses.

Sterilization

The most important thing Karol learned when studying the process of piercing is that cleanliness is of the utmost importance. She knows that every item which is needed (or may be needed) must be sterilized. "Even disposable piercing needles must be sterilized before they are used," she emphasizes, "and in the unlikely event that pliers would be needed to push together a ring which has been twisted out of shape, these, too, should be sterile."

Jewelry

The selection of jewelry is important. The jewelry must be made of stainless steel or gold. Besides rings and hoops in different sizes, spikes, arrows, studs, and tusks are offered. Sometimes gemstones are attached to the fittings. Regular earrings are not appropriate for other parts of the body, such as noses, eyebrows, navels, or nipples. Jewelry made for ear piercing is of too small a gauge to work in body piercing. Body piercing jewelry is usually shaped as either a hoop or a barbell, which is a straight cylinder, capped at both ends with a detachable ball.

Body piercing jewelry comes in a variety of gauges. Most noses are pierced with eighteen-gauge needles, while navels require the slightly larger gauge of sixteen or fourteen. The body has a natural instinct to rid itself of foreign objects, and piercing jewelry is no exception. If the jewelry is too narrow, it can be pushed out.

The Piercing Process

Karol explains a piercing session: "A young woman, Toni, decided to have her navel pierced. She wanted a small hoop centered on the bottom rim of her belly button. I autoclaved a hoop, a pair of Pennington forceps (which look like scissors with hollow spoons on the tips), a sixteen, gauge needle and opened an individually-packaged cork. These are the tools used for piercing. Before the piercing I lowered the shades on the connecting window between the tattoo room and the waiting area. Piercing is a personal choice and a private act. I strongly feel it is wrong for other customers to observe this process.

"Next, I wash my hands and put on a pair of disposable latex gloves. I carefully cleaned the skin

around Toni's navel with betadine soap before I began the piercing procedure. Toni stood very straight as I knelt in front of her, visually identifying the proper location for the hoop. After I made a small dot with a pen, Toni examined it in the full-length mirror. She approved of the placement and then seated herself in the reclining dentist's chair I use for tattoos and piercing. From the autoclave, I removed the forceps and the needle and wiped a thin coating of Neosporin ointment on the needle. Neosporin is an antibiotic substance, which lubricates the needle so that it glides through the skin as quickly as possible.

"Aligning the dot on Toni's skin inside the open circle of the forceps, I squeezed them shut until they locked. Not surprisingly, Toni shut her eyes and gripped the arms of the chair. 'You're doing great,' I said to encourage her, and because I knew what she was experiencing. I placed the cork on the underside of the forceps, and held the needle above the dot, almost touching the skin. 'We'll do it on three, okay?'

"I counted to three and then pushed the needle quickly through Toni's skin. She breathed deeply and opened her eyes, looking down at the needle which was piercing her skin. 'There's no blood,' she said and sounded surprised. The skin around the needle was beginning to redden, but she was right. There is rarely any blood in a piercing which is professionally done.

"After that, I tucked the end of the hoop into the open end of the needle and told her, 'The worst part is over.' I pushed the needle and hoop through the hole I'd made in the skin, removed the needle from *the jewelry, and twisted the ends of the ring until they were aligned. Toni said she was feeling fine and after I dabbed both sides of the piercing with betadine and applied a dab of Neosporin, I handed her a copy of the after-care instructions."*

Is It Painful?

The amount of pain a person feels during a piercing depends on a few things. It can depend on the fact that everyone has his or her own individual pain threshold. What is extremely painful for you may be bearable for someone else. It can also depend on what body part is pierced. Since the skin of the nose is so thick, many piercers report that nose piercings can be very painful. Some body parts are more sensitive than others, such as the nipples or the genitals.

Taking Care of the Piercing

These instructions are very specific. Toni, for instance, was told not to immerse the piercing in water for a month. She must wash the area several times a day with an antibacterial soap and often work the hoop back and forth through the opening so that the healing skin does not stick to the metal. It is important to wear loose clothing until the piercing heals.

After Toni read the instructions, Karol cautioned her to call immediately if there were any redness or infection around her piercing. Next, Toni signed a release form which says that she has read the instructions, that she understands the instructions, and that she will follow the instructions. It also says that the piercing was properly conducted in a sterile setting and that she is responsible for any infection or problems that might occur as a result of her failure to adhere to the instructions. This release form protects the shop in case of a lawsuit. A piercer will have his or her customers read and sign it to reinforce the importance of taking care of the piercing.

How Long Does It Take to Heal?

A piercing takes a lot of care. In the beginning, it may be swollen, itchy, red, and tender. Crusting around the piercing is also common. Piercings should be cleaned but not more than twice a day. Cleaning too much could damage skin cells. Cleaning too little could invite an infection.

People heal at different rates, but most healing periods for piercings are a year. Healing rates also depend on the thickness of the skin. The earlobe, eyebrow, and septum will take six to eight weeks, and the ear cartilage and nostril will take two to twelve months. In some areas, a healed piercing is not visible. If you decide to let a piercing grow back together, it may leave no more than a small dent on the skin. Some piercings, which grow back together in an earlobe, an ear cartilage, a nostril, or a lip often look like little white lumps. Many people believe that if they take a piercing out, it won't be noticeable at all. This is not always true. There is really no way to tell what the skin will look like if a person decides to remove the piercing.

Sometimes, the piercing doesn't heal properly. The body may reject the piercing, and it has to be taken out soon after the procedure is done.

Helen thought about getting her nose pierced for about three months. After she felt she was absolutely sure about her decision, she made the appointment. She was warned against having any caffeine, aspirin, or alcohol the day of the procedure and to make sure she ate beforehand.

At the shop, they checked her driver's license, and she had to sign a waiver. The procedure was explained in detail before anything happened. The piercer took a pen and marked the spot on Helen's nose. Helen checked it in the mirror to make sure she liked the placement. The piecer put on surgical gloves and he opened up the needle, which was sterilized, along with all the other equipment. He told her to take a deep breath in, and he would do the piercing as she exhaled. Helen felt a lot of resistance as the needle went through the skin. "It was incredibly painful. There was a lot of blood because I had drunk some coffee that morning, even though I knew I wasn't supposed to. I felt as if all the muscles in my face were contracting all at the same time because of the pain. My eyes involuntarily teared. The piercer said that happens with everybody. It took a few minutes for the bleeding to stop."

Helen had problems from the very beginning. "I got it done in January, and by March it was still very painful to the touch, and it was still oozing a clear, yellowish liquid. At one point, I had to go on antibiotics for the infection. The doctor told me to take the nose ring out, but I wanted to wait and see what would happen. The antibiotics got rid of the infection, but as *soon as I went off the medication, the infection came back. Finally, I had to take the nose ring out in April. I was fed up, and it hurt all the time."*

Health Risks

Dr. Kayenta Thompson works in a skin clinic. "I don't like today's piercing and tattooing fad because of the potential damage," she says. "These practices could mean an irreparable scarring to a person's body. I have seen piercings done from professional shops as well do-it-yourself handiwork. Everyone says the needles that they use are sterile, but that's not always true."

Dr. Thompson says that some common body piercing complications include staph infections and contact dermatitis which is often picked up from the nickel composition of the piercing jewelry. Dermatitis is an allergic reaction to a substance that comes into repeated contact with the body. When it develops, the pierced area won't heal, and the skin festers, swells, and gets sore.

"Pull-through injuries, where jewelry gets hooked on something, can also be a problem. Eyebrow pull-through, where the jewelry ripped out of the hole, often requires plastic surgery," Dr. Thompson says. The whole situation can be time consuming, costly, and painful."

A few years ago doctors and skin specialists began seeing a rise in problems related to body piercing. Inadequate sterilization, lack of technique, and allergic reactions to the nickel content in some jewelry can lead to infection and scarring.

Dr. Becky Botkin says, "To have a piercing in the tongue and wearing a screw and bolt are harsh on a person's teeth and gums. The teeth are easily cracked, chipped, or knocked out because the tongue is not easily controlled with the added weight of a spike or stud. Sometimes the roof of the mouth takes a beating, and cuts, scrapes, and sores appear. These abrasions can cause swelling and inflammation. If careful hygiene is not followed, infection sets in. Not long ago, I performed some costly and difficult dentistry on a young man. His front tooth had been sheared off by a large stainless steel bolt. My client required surgery, and it took three appointments to complete the job."

A Bill of Rights

Gauntlet, Inc., a professional piercing service, and the Association of Professional Piercers have drawn up a set of rules entitled "A Piercee's Bill of Rights." Every person has the right:

- ☞ to be pierced in a scrupulously hygienic, open environment, by a clean, conscientious piercer wearing a fresh pair of disposable latex gloves.

- ☞ to a sober, friendly, calm, and knowledgeable piercer, who will guide them through their piercing experience with confidence and assurance.

- ☞ to the peace of mind which comes from knowing that their piercer knows and practices the very highest standards of sterilization and hygiene.

- ☞ to be pierced with a brand-new, completely sterilized needle, which is immediately disposed of in a medical sharps container after use on the piercee alone.

☞to be touched only with freshly sterilized, appropriate implements, properly used and disposed of or resterilized in an autoclave prior to use on anyone else.

☞to know that ear-piercing guns are NEVER appropriate, and are often dangerous when used on anything other than ear lobes.

☞to be fitted only with jewelry which is appropriately sized, safe in material, design, and construction, and that best promotes healing. Gold-plated, gold-filled, and sterling silver jewelry are never appropriate for any new or unhealed piercing.

☞to be fully informed about proper aftercare and to have continuing access to their piercer for consultation and assistance with all their piercing-related questions.

Anyone who is considering a piercing should go to a shop that follows these rules. As with tattooing, it's important to investigate more than one shop and to give great consideration to your decision. You may feel that getting pierced is not a major decision. But there are many factors to consider, such as infection, pain and discomfort, as well as regret. If you decide to take out the piercing, you may be left with a scar as a constant reminder.

Branding

During the reign of Henry VIII (1491-1547), the English branded outcasts in varying places on their bodies, depending upon the crime. Cutpurses and pickpockets were branded with an "S" on the cheek. This letter, made with a hot iron, indicated "slave," and the accused was sent into a lifetime of indenture. Branding as a form of punishment and the identification of criminals was abolished in the eighteenth century.

The French, too, marked convicts with brands. A fleur-de-lis, a design of three iris petals tied by an encircling band, was branded into the shoulder of an accused. The symbol ostracized the offender, and he or she was forever shunned. Protestants were also branded as criminals. Eventually, so many French Huguenots wore the fleur-de-lis that the design lost its original meaning of "untouchable." Today, it is the national symbol of France.

Today, branding is the creation of raised scars on skin, and like tattooing, it is often considered a second skin. Similar to the popularity of tattooing and piercing, branding is showing up on more people's bodies and in more places.

Because of its nature, getting a brand may be more intense than most body modifications. Certainly, it captures the imagination because the words, "kiss of fire," "tip of fire," or "lick of fire" easily conjure up a touch of terror. Also, for some people this particular type of art may go beyond accepted cultural boundaries.

Some people do this form of body art to mark a rite of passage or to celebrate a special change in their lives. It can have a symbolic meaning to that person and his or her peers, or it may be done as a symbol of artistic self-expression. Many tribal people have puberty initiations that involve branding. Men and women, young and old, sometimes explain that being branded has a dramatic effect that empowers them. Many practitioners state that for them branding is full of spirituality and fulfillment.

According to the Bible and in the book of Genesis, God placed a mark on the earth's first murderer before sending him into exile. The mark of Cain, perhaps a "flash of fire," forever branded the brother of the slaughtered Abel as a criminal and outcast.

Mass murderer, Charles Manson, and his followers had brands on their foreheads during the 1970-71 sensational Skelter Trials. When Manson was escorted into the courtroom, people were horrified. During the night Manson had taken a sharp object and carved a bloody swastika on his forehead. Over the weekend, killers, Susan Atkins, Patricia Krenwinkel, and Leslie Van Houten lit matches, heated bobby pins red-hot, and then burned swastikas on their foreheads. To create more prominent scars, they split open the burnt flesh with needles. Later, Sandy, Squeaky, Gypsy, and other Manson Family members did the same. The brands were always the first thing people saw when the group was brought into court. This was graphic evidence that when Manson led, the girls followed. As new groupies joined this flock, branding became one of their rituals.

The word "brand" has several definitions, such as logo, seal, or trademark, but frequently it means a mark that is made by burning. When a person hears the word "branding," he or she is most likely to think of movies and videos showing the wild West, trail rides, and cattle roundups. For generations, ranchers have branded calves as a means of showing ownership. This is done on the rib cage, hip, or shoulders. Veterinarians also tattoo show horses in the lower lip for identification and pierce the ears of sheep and cows for repellent tags to ward off flies.

With cattle, the procedure involves branding irons that are placed on a fire. When the iron glows white with heat, it is ready for use. On high-tech ranches, an electric branding iron, similar in appearance to a curling iron, is often used. The technique for branding cattle does not work well on human bodies because the areas are smaller and have more curvature than the flank of a cow.

"To keloid," a colloquial modification of the word keloid, means to create raised scars. Keloiding is related to the amount of melanin, the dark pigment in the epidermis. The darker the skin, the better the keloid. Many African-American fraternities have a long tradition of branding new pledges as an initiation rite. The brand is usually in the shape of one of the fraternity's Greek letters and is meant to be visible for life. The Rev. Jesse Jackson has such a brand, as does Emmit Smith of the Dallas Cowboys. Smith's brand, a "sigma" on his left biceps, is visible in most photographs.

Richard is a wide receiver on a state university football team. Earlier in his school career, he joined the Kappa Alpha PSI Fraternity. "My father was a member of this group when he went to college," Richard says, "so the brotherhood is meaningful to both of us."

As a sophomore, Richard joined fifteen other young men in a ritual branding. "The members lent support, and it was fun," Richard says. "The man that did the branding understands the process and knows what he's doing. He has a book where he keeps the names of his 100-200 clients and makes notes where the brandings are given. The usual places are on the calf, chest or bicepses."

Richard's branding was done on the kitchen countertop at the fraternity house. The different brands were heated on an electric stove. Richard says he was the fifth or sixth person to be branded. His arm was first rubbed with alcohol, and he received the strike on his left biceps. The brand, a floating "K" in a diamond shape, was made from a one-piece iron. The brand was tapped on for maybe less than a second.

"It's called 'giving hits," Richard explains, "and it made a terrible stink, like burning bacon. I'd say that the smell was the worst part because it didn't hurt that bad. Afterward, I felt giddy and excited. The next morning, I woke up without pain.

"At first, the brand sort of sinks into the arm, and there's a lot of dead skin in the healing. I had this constant need to touch it. I used peroxide two or three times a day and didn't use Neosporin as sometimes suggested. I didn't want the burn to heal and not leave the mark. The hair on my upper arm turned white from peroxide, but there was no infection. It *was a constant effort not to pick the scab, but I was determined that it would come out clean." The brand is now healed and not distorted in any way. Richard says that his mom had mixed feelings about his branding but did say that it looked nice. He also says that his father understands but does not plan to follow in his branded footsteps.*

Richard knows that branding is not for everyone. "My brand means a life-long commitment to my fraternity. It gives me strength and reminds me to never settle for less. Sometimes, I rub my arm when I'm in a football game and that helps me to play harder. In fact, I'm going to have another brand at a later date. The next time, I plan to have it placed on my right calf."

How Is Branding Done?

Branding is done by taking a white hot metal shape, and pressing it onto flesh. This motion is called a strike. A completed design is usually made up of separate but multiple strikes of the branding tool. Each strike becomes a scar, which makes up a section of the design. The finished brand looks like a pattern of thick raised lines.

While branding may sound easy, it is not something to be attempted without giving it a lot of thought. Doing this on the spur-of-the-moment in a bedroom, in the garage, or in a basement is unlikely to produce anything more than a miserable burn, and an unattractive scar. The decision shouldn't be made at a party, a festival, or a beer bust.

Unprofessional brandings can be dangerous. Ordinary objects, such as coat hangers and paper clips, are not suitable for use as branding tool and can produce unsightly blisters and uneven scars. The same goes for soldering irons because they are too blunt and often do not produce a uniform line when drawn across the skin. Wires do not hold heat long enough to make a clean strike. Cattle branding irons make burns that are too wide and too deep for human designs. Copper and brass strips are generally too soft and lose their shape when heated red hot. It is important that the iron retains heat long enough to make a clean, even strike.

Branding should be performed only by people who have studied the art of body modification, know the anatomy of the body, and understand the procedure of body branding. It is necessary for the brander to be steady-handed, clear-headed, and physically accurate. The brander should wear hygienic gloves and work in a clean environment.

Steel strips, tin-can metal, and heavy sheet metal are suitable materials with which a professional brander can make into brand pieces.Other tools that are sometimes used for branding are medical cauterizing lasers and stainless-tipped cauterizers. Artists also have good results with silver objects and metal objects, such as spikes, bolts, clamps, and screws. Ceramic pieces are also used. Irons should always be sterilized in an autoclave. Steel wool should be used to clean the brand or brand pieces.

Designs

Skillful artists know the spacing of a design is important. Multiple strike designs need to be carefully planned out on paper before shaping the iron. Many professional branders insist that a brand piece be made one inch or less in length and that the design be kept simple. Brands spread two to three times wider than the hot metal used to make them. The brand pieces are designed with allowance for spreading.

One way a craftsman makes initials, complex monograms, or symbols, is to use multiple strikes of basic shapes. Unlike tattoos, branding pieces do not execute detailed or intricate designs. Nonetheless, metal in the shapes of straight lines, right angles, horseshoes, arcs, half moon, checks, semi-circles, slight curves, and dots, are struck into intricate patterns and complex geometric designs.

Other patterns that can be formed by professional branders include designs of a sun, rocky road, snake, or whip, lightning, chain, flower, snowflake, rainbow, animal, animal tracks, and trailing vine. Before being used on a subject, the branding piece is heated and tested on a piece of cardboard, a raw potato, or an uncooked chicken breast to show the client what it will look like. This may also give the client an idea of what happens when a hot strike hits flesh.

"Frankly, I like to rattle cages and shake people up," says Gwen. "I have several tattoos on my back and two barbells in my tongue. I also have a gold ring in my lower lip, and starting at the top of my right ear, I have studs running down to the lobe. I also shave my head. Branding didn't appeal to me until a friend showed me an initial, "W," that he had branded on his backside. He told me that every strike was pure

hell, and that he yelled a lot and there's no worse odor than the smell of burning flesh.

"After talking to this guy, I felt that I knew what I would be in for when I finally opted for having a brand. I chose a design at the top of my right biceps, an armband made with thirty-six strikes.

"The really tough time was the aftercare. It caused me misery every day of the three months it took for the imprint to heal. With this brand, I consider myself truly a modern primitive."

Placement

Branding professionals say the best location for a brand is on a flat surface of the body and away from bones and vital organs. The smallest curvature on the area being struck will cause the brand to burn deeply in some spots, lightly, or not at all in others. In parts of Africa, where branding is used as decoration or ritual initiation, the areas most branded are the upper chest, breast, upper back, shoulders, upper arms, thighs, flat areas of the belly, and flat sides of the calves. Placing a brand in these areas increases the chance of a clear impression.

Getting the "Lick of Fire"

It's extremely important that the artist be an expert at judging placement and correct temperature. It's also imperative to know the length of time that the steel is held to the skin, and the use of proper pressure. The heated tool should be held on the skin no longer than a second or two. Not pushing hard on the iron should result in a light scar.

Some brandees insist that the pain lasts only the short time that the flesh is being burned away. Others say that the agony is fleeting and that they feel clear, calm and spiritual. Clients also tell about being able to step aside from their body for the thirty to sixty minutes it takes to complete a more complicated design. Because of the intense sensation of the branding strikes, pain-relieving chemicals are secreted in the brain that have an effect like that of morphine. When the endorphins kick in, the client gets a rush. Consequently, the emotional impact of being burned does strange things to the body and psyche. During a multistrike brand session, it is normal for everyone present to feel high. As a result of the excitement, it's easy for people to get hooked on the process.

Caring for a Brand

How the brand is cared for will affect the finished result. There are risks of infection, as with all body art, but this can be minimized with good care. Usually, aloe vera gel and nonstick pads are used to dress brands after they are completed. It is usually suggested that, during the healing period, the flesh surrounding the branded area should be cleaned twice a day with alcohol gel or Betadine. Because different things work for different skin types, a person should be aware of what soap, lotion, salve, disinfectant, and medication his or her skin responds to. During the long healing period, the brand will be very sore, especially if it is on a body part that flexes.

The danger of infection comes as the scab develops. If the scab cracks, it can become an entry for bacteria.

Second, and third, degree burns are easily infected. Most brands are considered to be third-degree burns.

After a month or two, the brand shows signs of healing. In the beginning, the brand is covered with a scab, which ultimately falls away. Next, it becomes a ruby-colored scar. In time, it becomes a pink shade, and eventually, it becomes lighter than the brandee's normal skin tone. At approximately six months, a burn should be completely healed. In the end, a permanent mark, a brand, remains.

Danger, Danger, Danger

Just because tattooing, body piercing, and branding are the current trend, doesn't mean they are safe. It's necessary to know about these procedures before getting involved. Branding, an extreme form of body decoration, is not a precise art, and there are only a few artists with experience. Consistent results are difficult to achieve by even someone who is considered skillful.

Some advocates suggest that picking at scabs of a brand's healing tissue greatly increases the chances of the desired effect. However, body branding is far from an exact science. Picking or irritating a scab could end up as uneven scarring. Even more possible, a terrible infection or disease could develop. An allergic reaction to the procedure is also probable.

Trying to brand on your own could easily result in severely burning yourself or causing serious damage to your body. An example: a person might use hot paper clips as a rehearsal for getting a brand. Bits of chrome or another kind of plating could be left on the skin. This could mean that bits of metal would have to be removed from the skin which would be a difficult and uncomfortable procedure. An allergy or chemical irritation could result. It could mean the expense of antibiotics or even hospitalization.

Sometimes, liquid nitrogen is used to brand cattle. To do this, the hair is clipped from the animal where the brand is to be made on the skin. The liquid chemical is super-cold and immediately freezes the tissue. Commonly, a number is branded on the jaw of the animal. Eventually, the cow's hair grows out as a white brand or mark of identification. Recently, people have been experimenting by using liquid nitrogen for branding their bodies. Liquid nitrogen is difficult to obtain, difficult to store, and dangerous to use. Professionals do not use this method.

Branding appears to be the latest craze in a series of body modification practices that get more and more shocking. As more people explore the possibilities of body art, the risks and dangers increase. What was outrageous and offensive ten years ago seems familiar and normal today. Some people are always looking for a way to separate themselves from the mainstream. For some, tattooing and piercing are not radical enough anymore. They are looking for something different and exciting. In the same way that a mountain climber keeps looking for a bigger peak to conquer, some want to indulge in body art that pushes the limits of acceptability and cultural standards.

Because branding involves fire and burning, it is something to really think seriously about before you get involved. One of the main considerations is that it's such a new practice there aren't any organizations to regulate the proper procedures. As you've read earlier, the key to considering any body art is to investigate. But information on branding isn't easy to find. It's best that anyone interested talk with many different people, doctors and parents included, before making a decision. While a brand can be removed by laser, it is very time consuming, painful, and expensive. Consider the time it takes for a burn victim to recover from a fire. Even with great care and medication, many scars remain.

Tattooing, Piercing, and Branding Artists

At one time Samuel M. Steward, Ph.D., was a university professor. Art was an interest, and over the years, he wrote several hundred short stories. Under the pseudonym of Phil Andros, he wrote mysteries and erotic novels. A man of countless talents, he was a researcher for Dr. Alfred Kinsey, famed for his Institute for Sex Research.

At one point in his life, Sam Steward became disenchanted with academia and decided to become a tattoo artist. In his book, *Bad Boys and Tough Tattoos* he tells about sending for a correspondence course from the "only school of its kind in existence," to learn the art. "In the past," he writes, "there was only one publicized ad for tattooing...Zies, the School For Tattooing (by mail). This ad was in the back of *Mechanix Illustrated.*"

The lessons came mimeographed and bound in orange paper. Steward explains that the person who wrote the lessons knew little about tattooing and that the assignments were dull. Nevertheless, the course was duly completed, and the ex-teacher opened a studio. For many years, Steward tattooed under the name of Phil Sparrow. He describes his life as very different from the one he had known as a world traveler, writer, and friend of the famous. For a while, Sam/Phil went on teaching during the days, and tattooing on weekends. Eventually, his interest in tattooing won over. He also made more money in a day as a tattoo artist than in a month teaching at a university.

Phil does say he learned a few things from the correspondence course but not much. He really learned his craft from an old master tattooist in Milwaukee. "Tattooing," he says, "seems to be one of the few remaining skills that must be passed from a master to an apprentice."

Today, tattooing, piercing, and branding are not what a lot of people expect. For one thing, there may be close to 100,000 people in the United States making a living as tattooists, piercers and branders. More women are entering the tattooing and piercing profession.

Many of these staff members have studied at respected art schools or have degrees from distinguished universities. For most artists, it is a far more lucrative business to work in a tattoo studio than in an art studio where his or her painting may or may not sell. The tattooing of a large back piece, leg piece, or arm sleeve can easily cost $150.00 an hour. At one time, tattoo shops were managed by men only. It was unusual for a woman to request a tattoo and a rarity to ask for a piercing or brand, let alone to run a shop. Today, women account for almost 50 percent of professional tattooists.

In many magazines, there are advertisements offering correspondence lessons and workshops to learn about tattooing and piercing. One recent ad reads, "If you can trace, you can tattoo." This is false advertisement. Commercial ads usually start out with, "You too can make big money." The fact is that the person offering the course is the only one who makes money.

Hairdressers sometimes offer the service of ear piercing. Recent magazine advertisements suggest that men and women working in this trade can also increase their business by learning how to do permanent make-up. The following is an example of such an ad.

ATTENTION: An opportunity such as this comes by once in a lifetime. Because you are the owner of a beauty salon, you have the clientele and we have the knowledge. We can teach you how you can triple your business.

Learn about applying permanent cosmetics: eyebrows, eye-liner, and upper and lower lip liner. We can teach you this method in a two to three day seminar—and you get an accredited diploma. We teach all forms of tattooing and color analysis. With our method, you will be able to cover stretch marks on men's bodies and ladies, breasts and thighs. Having this knowledge should increase your business ten times profit-wise.

Our price for this course is a mere one thousand dollars and includes the equipment you will need. This is the first time this is offered at this sensational price. Don't wait!

Fact and Fiction

While this ad is persuasive, it is not truthful. Learning how to tattoo designs is an art form that takes time, patience and extreme skill. It is unlikely that it can be taught or learned by mail. To be a credible tattooist, he or she must have skill, do research, and become educated to the needs of clients. A man or woman can develop this career best by being an apprentice to a professional tattooist. As an apprentice, the student will learn how to buy materials, work a tattoo machine, and use colors.

The Tattoo Apprentice

In years past, artists were secretive about the technique of giving tattoos. They did not share ideas or information about procedures. Anyone who tried to break into the field was discouraged. Artists would not answer questions. Back then, anyone interested in learning the trade would hang around tattoo shops. If he (girls and women had not yet entered the field) were lucky, he became mop-up boy, and he'd eventually get to learn from the master. In time, he would catch on about soldering needles to the needle bar and how to outline and shade a tattoo. Back then, shops were located in the seedy parts of the city or near a wharf if located in a coastal town.

Today, a six-month apprenticeship costs a student approximately $1500. This may include written as well as oral instructions and use of the shop owner's inks, autoclave, and machinery. The beginner will observe the master tattooist at work and learn how to apply stencils and to utilize flash. The student also learns necessary information, such as that a tribal design is composed of thick black lines and that a Celtic tattoo is composed of knot work. Most important is learning how to hold and use the necessary tools. It takes effort to get used to the weight of the tattoo gun and understand how to apply pigment to skin in order to execute a good tattoo.

The Tattoo Machine

A tattoo machine is small, delicate, and lightweight. It rests easily in a normal-size palm. It can be compared to a dental drill. It is made of stainless steel, and with the power pack, cords and needle tube, it weighs six to eight ounces. A foot pedal turns the power off and on, and the instrument is held like a writing pen. The number of punctures per minute is controlled by a rheostat which is regulated by the tattooist's thumb. Two machines are used for tattooing, one for making outlines and another for shading.

Connected to the power pack is the needle bar. The attached needles look like delicate bristles on an expensive paint brush. Holding the skin taut and wearing hygienic gloves, the tattooist stretches the skin and outlines a design. Outlines are made at a higher speed (more punctures per minute) than shading and coloring.

Tattoo Inks

Tattoo shops have access to a variety of inks. They range in price from cheap to an expensive $15.00 per half ounce. Powdered pigment, which is mixed with distilled water, glycerin, and vodka, is relatively inexpensive. Unfortunately, these colors blur and fade as the liquid elements leach into the surrounding cells. This leaves dry powder beneath the skin. Predispersed inks are pigments suspended or dissolved in a gelatin-like base. Tattoo artists dilute this with distilled water. This ink, purchased from catalogs or specialty shops, lasts longest and holds its shape best in the skin. The tattooist constantly makes use of a smear of Vaseline to sooth the skin and successfully embed ink into the client's skin.

As a student, Dale won several prizes for his art work. "The truth is my tattoos sell easier than my art work," he confides. "My interest and knowledge of art made me curious about tattoos." Dale has managed a tattoo and piercing shop for a year. "An important thing I learned is that inferior ink makes bad tattoos. They fade and look tacky. Success for a good tattoo is often determined in the quality of the ink."

The Tattoo Artist

A professional tattooist will not be surprised at any unusual design he or she may be asked to produce. Neither will they be unnerved by the requested placement of the design. This ability to be almost shock-proof is part of the job, and a good tattooist is usually able to handle most situations. However, a sign on the door of The Purple Dragon announces that: "We charge extra for tattooing difficult areas." A reader would correctly assume that means regions such as the bikini line, genitalia on men or women, the stomach, and women's breasts. Here, the skin is more difficult to stretch properly and takes longer to tattoo.

"A tattooist will have all kinds of experiences, good, bad, and ugly," Jason says. "One of the worst situations I ever had was when a client stopped breathing. Of course, I thought it was because he was frightened, but actually a terrible attack of the flu struck him just at the time I started to tattoo. I called the paramedics, and he spent a few days in the hospital. When he completely recovered, he came back to the shop for his tattoo." Jason remembers that the funniest experience was when an angry mother showed up because Jason had tattooed her son. "Really mad," he says. "When I explained that her son was of legal age, and I was just doing my job, she cooled off. In fact she even managed to laugh a bit."

Body Piercers

Many professional tattooist are piercers as well. The main instrument of this trade is an assortment of different sized medical needles which look like hypodermic syringes. Tattoo studios stock rubbing alcohol to clean skin areas and an autoclave to sterilize their piercing equipment which include pliers and forceps. Iodine is used to clean places, such as the skin folds of a belly button or an ear flap. Included in the piercing supplies are skin scribes and pens which are used for marking ring openings for jewelry.

"All customers who get piercings must sign a waiver form," said a manager at a piercing studio. If the person is under eighteen years old, a parent must sign as well. We always give out instructions for tattoo and piercing care, but some clients don't take it seriously. Following directions for care is of the utmost importance if the tattooing or piercing is to be successful."

The Blacksmith

Leonard is a blacksmith. His shop has a concrete floor and a pot belly stove for heat. Outside his shop is an 1895 forge and an anvil. He works year-round but never in high wind. "That's dangerous," he says.

Although it is a simple operation, Leonard, a retired

policeman, says that he makes a fair-to-good living. Part of the satisfaction for Leonard is when he and his wife, April, show their wares at craft shows and bazaars.

This blacksmith specializes in designing and making hand-forged knives and western accessories, such as dinner bells and barbecue forks. In fact, his output consists of over 300 items, including door knockers, letter holders, and napkin holders. He also designs brands. "These are mostly for horses and cows," he says.

Recently, Leonard made a one-piece zodiac sign for a man named Swatch. Swatch was hired by a group that wanted to do body branding. The brand that Leonard forged will join the hundred-plus branding irons that Swatch has in his unique collection. Swatch has been a tattooist since the 1960s. In the late 1970s he started piercing, and at the end of the 1980s, he started branding. "Young people kept coming into my shop and asking about what they called 'slash and burn' and I got interested."

Consulting a blacksmith, Swatch supervised the creation of his first brand, a straight half-inch piece. He then practiced branding on wood, cardboard, and sometimes a potato. "I practiced making lines, a triangle, or a star," he says. "After a while, I was able to make even strokes. I even started making small burn marks on myself. It didn't hurt as much as a person would expect. The important part is not burning too deep. With tattooing, you're getting something put into your skin. With branding, the skin becomes embossed. It seems more natural.

"Some of my irons are one piece: a half-moon, a circle, and a straight line. I often combine several of *these pieces to make a strong design. Branding a strike at a time is more time-consuming and complicated, but the most successful."*

In the beginning, one or two customers per month requested brands. As he became known as a professional brander, business picked up. His first request for a group branding came from a fraternity located in Chicago. The brothers wanted to be branded as personal statements of loyalty to their fraternity and each other. Eventually, his name became known among black college fraternities in the South. As requests grew for his work, so did his collection of branding irons. "Fraternities have their own more intricate logos and prefer a one-piece brand that has a complete design," Swatch says. "This type of branding iron takes only one 'hit' and works well on dark skin. The process takes seconds."

He also explains that the process is fairly simple. "In my studio, I use a blowtorch to heat the instrument. At a frat house, I heat the iron over the jet of the kitchen's gas stove. Either one works fine. A simple application, which includes preparation, the branding, and directions about the aftercare, requires a fifteen-minute sitting or standing and costs the client about $50. If a fraternity is a long distance, I charge air-fare. That sounds like a lot of money is involved. It is. However, because these rituals are dignified, serious, and well-thought out, branding, for me is more rewarding than just money."

While branding is still a little-known art form, it's out there, and people are becoming more and more interested. Anyone considering a brand should consult with a professional brander. They're out there, too. Most likely, a tattoo artist and piercer can give a person the name of someone who does professional branding. Too often, branding is done on the spur-of-the-moment, creating a life-long regret. Luke, a senior in high school, has such a story.

"When I was seventeen, I got branded because I was with guys, and when guys get together they bond because they think they are going to be friends forever. Well, we were headed out one night and started talking about branding. It was getting popular with high school kids . . . lots of them have brands. They do the work themselves. In fact, there are kids at our school who have scars all down the side of their chests. Anyhow, we went to a friend's house and shaped coat hangers into the letters 'B,' 'N,' and 'L' for Brad, Neil, and Luke. We heated up a propane torch and then got our hanger initials red-hot. When the iron started to cool, we branded each other. We tried to be careful to take the iron off before it cooled because we knew that it would jerk off the skin.

"We did my brand too deep, and now it's a big, thick scar, like an orange slice. It's shaped like a fat sea horse, or the number two, or a huge question mark. The color is white and pink, and parts of it have sensitive stretch marks.

"At the time, my mom was mad because she felt I was destroying my skin, and that I wasn't thinking, and that I wouldn't want this brand in the next ten years. She felt that I was still her child and getting the brand was a rebellion thing. My dad agreed.

"My brand doesn't bother me except when I get

bumped or someone gives me a little pat on my upper arm. Then there's a sharp pain like a sting. If there were a way to take it off . . . lessen the disfiguration, I'd do it. When my girlfriend asked me about the blob on my arm, I told her that it was from a welding accident. I'm not exactly proud of my brand, and I didn't want to tell her the story."

A Professional Brander

Raelyn has done professional branding for eight years. "I brand all kinds of people and they are usually young. I've also done a few fraternity groups. My charge is $120 per hour, and most clients request an arm band. Not long ago, I place a Chinese character that stood for fertility on a woman who wanted a baby. It was branded on her abdomen.

"As a professional brander I take my work seriously. Branding has a lasting effect if it's done right. A professional brander has to know what he or she is doing. In my studio a client can't choose a design from a book or pluck one off the wall. If someone wants a brand, he or she needs to go to the library, do research, and take responsibility for what they want on their body. I do not brand the initials of friends or lovers for clients. Many relationships don't last. I feel that it is okay to question my clients about the reason they wish to be branded."

There are many different types of people who become tattoo, piercing, and branding artists. Many have strong opinions about their art and how they practice it. If you know a lot about their training, their equipment, and their personalities, you can decide if they are right for you. Some people prefer to work with female artists, saying they are less intimidating. Others don't care about gender, saying that their main concern is skill and price. Either way, if you've decided to get a tattoo, a piercing, or a brand, finding the right person to perform the procedure is essential. You are putting your trust, your body, and your money into that person's hands. If you don't feel comfortable working with one person, keep looking until you find an artist you like.

Laws and Regulations

As more tattoo, piercing, and branding studios open in the United States, more people are becoming concerned with health and safety regulations. There are no federal laws in existence concerning any of these procedures. Some states have no such laws, and others only regulate according to age, making it against the law to tattoo, pierce, or brand anyone under eighteen years of age without parental consent. Many states are trying to make changes. Tattooing has been outlawed in Connecticut, Florida, Kansas, Massachusetts, Oklahoma, South Carolina, Vermont, and Albuquerque, New Mexico.

In Florida, State Representative Carlos Valdes of Miami wants the state to require teens under the age of sixteen to have their parents' permission before getting anything but their earlobes pierced. He also wants to establish sanitation and sterilization standards for piercing. Mr. Valdes reports that parents have called from all parts of the nation, encouraging him to introduce such a bill.

In California, Senator Diane E. Watson is attempting to introduce a bill to minimize the transmission of diseases through tattooing, piercing, and other types of permanent cosmetics. She is calling on the state to establish health and safety standards for people conducting these types of businesses. The purpose is to protect consumers from the spread of disease from contaminated tools and supplies. Senator Watson is also looking to the State Department of Health Services to approve the standards and distribute them to all other county health departments should the bill pass into law.

The bill would require all practitioners of tattooing, piercing, and other permanent cosmetics to register with the county health department, follow the standards passed out by the county health department, and pay the appropriate fees. There would be a $500 fine for any business that violates the law, and all business would be subject to inspection at any time. In the past, similar bills have been vetoed by the governor. While the bill is supported by the California Medical Association, others feel that there is not enough evidence to support the idea that these businesses pose a public health problem.

There may be similar bills in your state, or laws may already exist for tattoo, piercing, or branding businesses. Contact your local health department to find out if such regulations exist. It's essential to deal only with practitioners who are registered.

Counter-Culture

Before tattooing became the vogue of the 1990s, most people associated it with the "outcasts" of society, such as prisoners and ex-cons, circus people, bikers, and gang members. Today, many use tattoos and piercings as symbols of their own personal rebellion.

Prisoners

Time hangs heavy for most convicts because there's not a lot to do in jails or prisons. Tattooing is generally forbidden. After lights are out, cellmates frequently and sometimes painfully tattoo one another. "In prison, it's important for a man to prove himself," an ex-convict says. "If he can get a tattoo it signals the other inmates that he can hustle the guards, get things done, and take care of himself."

Self-applied jail or penitentiary tattoos are usually crude in design. The amateur, or "scratcher," does not always know that the skin should be kept taut or the design will become a series of zigzags and wiggly lines, unattractive dots, or, most likely, a single splotch that is more a patch than a pattern.

Most often, the ink or color used to tattoo is made from carefully accumulated soot or from the soot of burned toilet paper, crumbled in water. Either way, the inmate gets pure carbon, which is the basis for the professional tattooist's black ink. However, the pure carbon, or any ordinary "India" ink that the inmate may manage to confiscate, is not stabilized with iron oxide. This is a necessary addition found in professional tattoo ink. Invariably, the prisoner's tattoo turns blue. Next, the prisoner steals needles, usually in the laundry where repairs are made on the prison uniforms. These are the tools that both male and female convicts use to tattoo. Prisoners often have word tattoos, such as "MOM," "DAD," "LOVE," and "HATE."

In the 1962 movie, *Cape Fear*, Robert Mitchum, playing the part of a criminal newly released from prison, used snarls and sneers to make him a "bad guy." In the 1991 remake of this same movie, Robert DeNiro, starring as the same character, has jailhouse tattoos all over his body. Words on his inner arm read, "VENGENCE IS MINE AND MY TIME IS AT HAND." On his back, he is tattooed with religious motifs designed to provoke horror from the movie audience. Brutal facial expressions are no longer enough to convince audiences of the character's evilness. DeNiro's modern anti-hero says, "Guess I've got too many tattoos, but there's nothing to do in prison but desecrate the flesh." This portrays him as a callous and cruel ex-con.

Jailhouse Tattoos

For security, prisoners in the county jail are not allowed anything that can be used as a weapon. Inmates are monitored by cameras twenty-four hours a day. Nonetheless, they manage to find a secluded area, usually the corner of their prison cell, to do tattooing. When inmates are presented with legal papers, they sometimes remove and conceal the staples and paper clips on their person. In their cell block or pod, away from cameras, they shave the lead from pilfered pencils or remove the ink from forbidden pens. This is mixed with water to make tattoo ink. The stolen staples or paper clips are straightened, inserted in a pencil eraser, and become a tattoo needle. The prisoner makes punctures on his or her skin and rubs in the cell-made ink.

Another technique for making the black-and-gray tattoos is using a pigment that is created from cigarette ashes. Commonly called "joint style," or "jailhouse" tattoos, these designs are punched in with a single needle or inferior machines, powered by a cassette-player motor. The results are crude and rough.

Police officers try to prohibit this behavior because consequences can be serious. "Not long ago," a sheriff reports, "an inmate tattooed himself using crude and unsanitary materials. The tattoo became infected. We had to rush him to the hospital, and he needed antibiotics for the rest of his incarceration. For safety, it's necessary to deny lawbreakers what most people use and take for granted."

Lt. Tom Perkins has been in the Albany County Sheriff's Department for fifteen years. He says that about 60 percent of the inmates have tattoos or other markings.

"As far as tattooing is concerned, being an inmate in a state or federal penitentiary is different from serving time in the county jail. Although the convicts in state or federal penitentiaries use staples and paper clips to make tattoo needles, they also have access to tape recorders and other mechanisms. They use parts and pieces of these to make

66

tattoo tools. At the prison store, they can purchase sewing needles, staples, and paper clips. Ink and paint are available. Because of this, tattooing, even though forbidden, is more difficult to control in state and federal prisons."

Gang Members

Gangs are prevalent worldwide. Tattooing, piercing, and branding are part of gang initiation rites. A spider web on the elbow indicates that the gang member has killed someone. Sometimes, an outlined teardrop near the right eye designates East Coast gangs, and an outlined teardrop near the left eye is for a West Coast member. A teardrop can also indicate that, as part of a gang initiation, the inducted member shot someone. The more tear drops that are tattooed, the more people he or she may have shot. Sometimes, a tattoo is of a female figure crying tears. These tears indicate the number of years the person has spent in jail. A tattooed web, dots, crosses, and "Xs" on the hand between the thumb and forefinger, are signature marks of gang associations.

Gang members, like much of society, are also interested in piercings and brandings. These forms of adornment have become a craze and take place as a ritual. Words, sayings, personal slogans, or the gang's name are burned on a gang member's back, chest, or belly.

Tattoo Removal for Former Gang Members

Some former members of gangs, as well as, some white supremacist organizations and neo-Nazi groups are having identifying tattoos, such as swastikas, removed. This is a costly thing to do. In some wealthy states, there are government programs and grants to pay for tattoo removal for former gang members who want to start a new life. Less wealthy states do not have the money to support such programs. A laser machine costs $100,000 plus the cost of operation, which includes a physician, nurse, and supplies.

Criminals turning state's evidence often ask that any identifying tattoos be removed. When a criminal turns state's evidence, he or she identifies other people who have committed certain crimes. This puts that person in great danger. When such people go into a protective program, the federal government customarily pays for everything that guarantees his or her safety. It is not unusual for a dermatologist to be contacted by government officials requesting tattoo removal for someone seeking a new identity.

Several states are trying to develop programs that will help gang members erase their identifiable tattoos. These programs are being offered in the hopes of curbing violence and helping members get out of gangs and into the work force. The plan involves vast amounts of money, time, and effort. Progress is slow. Not all taxpayers are willing to support such an expensive project.

People who wish to have tattoos removed in order to leave gangs are required to attend weekly support group meetings, have classroom training, do community service, and go to tattoo removal appointments. Volunteer physicians trained in laser surgery perform the treatments.

"One of the things that enables someone to get away from a gang is finding a decent job and getting on with his or her life," a volunteer nurse at a health clinic says. "A big challenge is the long-term follow-up of the youths after their tattoos have been removed."

"Sometimes," another nurse says, "a person turns around and gets another tattoo. Of course, this is discouraging to the youth's mentors, and certainly defeats the purpose of the program."

There have to be rules and requirements for any program. These may include completing a course on how to get a job, avoiding arrest for certain periods of time, and the willingness to sign a waiver promising not to get tattooed again. "We can't open a program free to just anyone," a volunteer nurse says. "It takes a serious screening process. We need doctors, plastic surgeons, and nurses who will give their time, money, and expertise. An expensive medical laser is necessary, too. It's a giant undertaking."

"Tattoo removal for gang members is cheaper in the long run," a volunteer plastic surgeon says. "These kids could spend the rest of their lives not contributing because they have tattoos and, of course, can't get jobs. To be unemployed could be a lifestyle of socioeconomic displacement. Surely, a program that will spend a couple hundred dollars to take off the youth-at-risk's tattoos is far cheaper than spending thousands a year warehousing someone in prison."

A Former Gang Member

Gino is seventeen years old and has several self-administered tattoos. He has a history of juvenile delinquency and is connected with a gang. His tattoos were made with various-sized needles and India ink. Recently, Gino decided that his life wasn't going any-

where. He sought counseling, entered into a rehabilitation program, and decided to break off with his gang alliance. This was not an easy thing for Gino, but he stuck it out in order to get his life back on a more reasonable track. Unfortunately, he has the markings of his earlier lifestyle. Because of his conspicuous tattoos, he feels he is a "marked man" in more ways than one.

Fortunately for Gino, there are doctors who volunteer their skills to help youth in trouble. Dr. Thaw was one of those people. He gave Gino laser removal treatments for nine months. "The treatments didn't hurt a lot," Gino says. "Mostly, it was scary, and it took a lot of time. It was embarrassing because there was no way I could ever pay for the treatments. Dr. Thaw was so nice, but he wasn't kidding when he told me I was never, never to mark up my body again."

After three more months of treatment, Gino's tattoos faded away. "It took a year of my time," he says, "and a lot of Dr. Thaw's time. I'm glad that my tattoos are gone. I just wish I hadn't tattooed myself in the first place."

Bikers

Bikers are men and women who ride the highways on motorcycles. Most ride Harley-Davidsons, also known as Hogs, which are made in America. Most bikers, some of whom have been in World War II, and many who have served in Korea or Vietnam, traditionally have many tattoos. The favorite tattoo among them is one of a bar-and-wings, the Harley-Davidson trademark. Another popular choice is a spider's web fanning out from the elbow.

Blondee has been Carrie's biker name since she was seventeen years old. She and her husband, Greg, ride Harley-Davidson motorcycles. Every chance they get, depending on the weather, they travel the highways of Colorado and Wyoming. They especially enjoy going to swap meets in Sturgis, South Dakota, where vendors and people who own Harley-Davidson dealerships sell motorcycle parts.

"Bikers are my family," Blondee says. "We have parties, barbecues, and picnics at the drop of a hat to celebrate anything. We go through joy and heartaches with one another. The laid-back lifestyle suits my nature."

Blondee has ten tattoos and three piercings in one ear and four in the other. She has nipple piercings, and so does her husband. "My tattooist does this," she says. "No branding. Branding is for punkers, not bikers." In the future Blondee plans to have more ear piercings and tattoos. "When I have an additional tattoo it will be one that expresses myself."

Blondee's first tattoo was a large bird of paradise on her shoulder. Her favorite is a tattoo created as a memorial to her mother. It is an underwater scene of the sea with fish, greenery, bubbles, and an oyster opening with a pearl. "Pearl was my mother's name, and beneath the tattoo are her birth and death dates."

Two other tattoos have special meaning for Blondee. One is the Harley-Davidson blue, red, yellow, and white emblem on her right shoulder which matches her husband's. The other, designed by Greg, is their marriage tattoo which is an Indian mandala, a shield with feathers. "We have our marriage tattoo on the same place on our shoulders so that there is room to grow. To celebrate our anniversary, we have beads added, and last year, Greg designed a shadow feather. He's an artist and has designed all of our tattoos."

For years, tattoos have adorned the arms and chests of people who consider themselves part of the counter-culture. Now, after decades of decline, tattoos are enjoying a rebirth among people in mainstream culture. At most bookstores and newsstands, body art magazines are for sale. In the majority of slick magazines, male models and beautiful women are shown with tattoos and piercings. As the world enters into the year 2000, tattoos, piercings, and sometimes brandings have become the vogue of America's youth. The question is: Will the rage of today be the outrage of tomorrow?

Pop Culture
Influences

It is difficult to find the answer to why a particular style, fashion, expression, or manner among groups of people becomes a trend. The fact is that popular fads never start from ground zero. According to one psychologist who studies pop culture, it is possible that military men of World War II set the foundation for the recent interest in tattooing, piercing, and branding.

Currently, many young people are curious about what the music, movies, fashion, and economy were like fifty years ago. During the war, a service man's A-2 jacket made a wonderful canvas for tattoo-style themes such as black cats, rolling dice, shamrocks, devils, tigers, grim reapers, and patch logos. Today, finding an original World War II A-2, brown leather flight jacket is next to impossible, but there are plenty of reproductions.

Ordinary collectibles of World War II such as wool army blankets, pea coats, flight jackets, trench shovels, and canteens, once sold in army surplus and second-hand stores, can no longer be found. Apparel and basic gear from that war are worth a lot of money. Occasionally, uniforms can be found at an estate or garage sale. Today, most military collectibles found in surplus stores are from the Korean, Vietnam, and Persian Gulf Wars. However, stories told by military men of the past and remembered by today's youths almost always include tales of how some-one, drunk or sober, was on leave and got a tattoo. "It was painful," Navy veteran, Morton May, remembers, "but it proved your endurance of pain and impressed your bud-dies." Morton also explains that in early times, if a sailor survived a ship that had gone down, they often had their ears pierced in memorial.

Other evidence of these tattoos exists in black-and-white war movies, documentary films, and the many recently pub-lished books about the armed forces of the past. At that time, body piercing and branding were part of the occult and secret organizations, not part of mainstream American culture.

Military Men

World War II was a difficult and prolonged conflict. For young, lonely soldiers with only a few hours of leave, it was something to do and someplace to go. The tattoo artist was often like a psychiatrist, best friend, priest, or the hometown barber. The tattooist was someone to whom they could con-fess their sins and tell intimate thoughts. For those young men, tattooing brought about much needed self-esteem and dignity. It bolstered ego, eased loneliness, and was consid-ered attractive to the opposite sex. It was also a possession no one could take away.

Fifty years ago, the most common tattoos that men in the military requested were anchors, hearts with "MOM," a girlfriend's name, and the American eagle. This was also a trend in the Korean and Vietnam Wars. The times have not changed much although many of today's service men request larger and more elaborate pieces of body art.

This tattoo covers the entire back and arms of a Vietnam veteran. It mimics the bold colors and designs made famous by ancient Japanese tattoo artists.

Some people decide to permanently honor their family's history by tattooing a family crest on their bodies.

Getting a tattoo with the name of a girlfriend or boyfriend may leave someone with an enormous sense of regret and embarrassment when the relationship ends.

This tattoo on the leg of a biker is an example of how many members of the counter-culture use body art to express their identity.

As the art of tattooing grows and becomes more popular, tattoo artists become more diverse. Today, many women play an important role in the tattoo artist community.

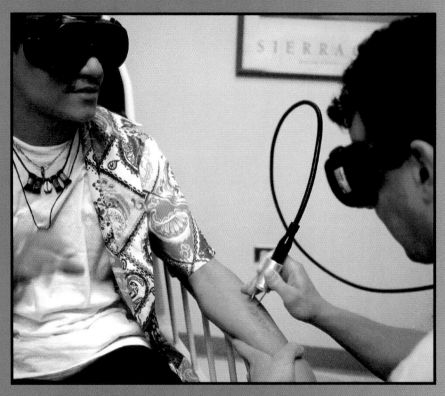

A former gang member undergoes laser surgery to remove the marks on his body. Protective goggles are worn by both the patient and the doctor during this procedure.

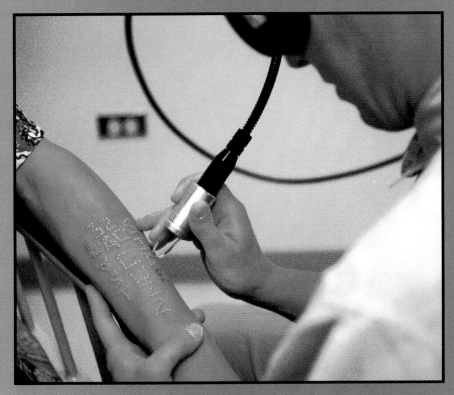

The laser machine uses light to break up the ink embedded in the skin. It can take several treatments and several hundred dollars to completely remove a tattoo.

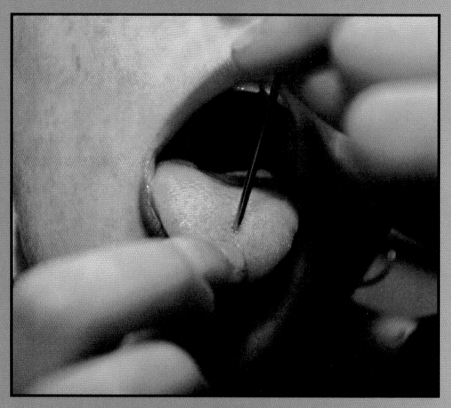

A tongue piercing can be difficult to handle because of the added weight of the jewelry. As a result, this kind of piercing causes dental problems, such as chipped teeth.

Many piercing artists say that the nose is one of the most painful places to pierce.

It is customary to make a stencil of the tattoo and place it on the body to show the client how it will look. This way a person can make changes before he or she is permanently marked.

As body piercing becomes more mainstream, some people search for ways to make their piercings different and more creative.

Many people who indulge in body art say that the process is addictive. It is rare for a person to have only one tattoo or piercing.

Celebrities can have a big influence on fashion trends. When Tommy Lee and Pamela Anderson got married, they tattooed wedding "bands" on their fingers.

Roseanne Barr removed the name of her ex-husband, Tom Arnold, from a tattoo on her body before she remarried her current husband.

Basketball star Dennis Rodman is known for his outrageous fashion choices. In addition to multi-colored hair, he has several tattoos and piercings.

Although branding is a new form of body art for mainstream culture, it is a traditional ritual for many African-American fraternities. Emmet Smith proudly shows his brand on and off the field.

Before and during WWII it was rare for women to have tattoos. It was not an interest of Woman's Army Auxiliary Corps
(WAAC) and Women's Appointed Volunteer Emergency
Service (WAVES), the female counterparts of the male Army
and Navy. In his book, *Bad Boys and Tough Tattoos*, Samuel
M. Steward, PhD, says that he did tattoo women who held
jobs as strippers and prostitutes. He also notes that one of the
most frequent questions asked by young servicemen who
patronized his shop was, "Do women ever come in here for
tattoos?" His answer was, "Yes, occasionally."

Certainly, since then, times have changed, and tattooing
has grown tremendously in the past decade. "Most people
of my generation will have tattoos," a teenager says as she
examines the flash on the wall of a tattoo studio. "Tattoos
look good and bring people together. It's a brotherhood
and sisterhood sort of thing."

> *Davey's uncle was an ex-Navy diver. When he was
> in the service he belonged to the SEALS, which is an
> acronym for Sea, Air and Land. After he retired he
> worked as an underwater welder. Recently Davey's
> uncle died. The family members wanted to honor his
> memory. After careful thought, they decided to get
> tattooed. On each relative's thigh,there is a deep sea
> helmet.*

The World of Fashion

The word "fashion" means "a prevailing custom or design
of dress." This definition covers a lot of territory. For style,
ancient Romans draped their tunics from the rings in their

nipple piercings. In Europe, Asia, and America, previous generations' pierced ears have always been a statement of elegance. The fashion business, a billion-dollar industry, promotes style for everyone—men, women, and children. Clothing, hairstyles, accessories, facial and body make-up are only a few of the specialties that this big business dictates. All the world believes that dress and ornamentation enhance the human body.

At one time tattoos were considered the marks of "lower-class" people. Tattoos are a lot more acceptable today than they were a generation ago. Because of this, piercing and tattooing do not seem as outrageous to people as they may have at one time. Today, the university professor and the glamorous prime-time newscaster probably have more up their sleeves than lectures and the latest news. Overall, however, people still consider branding a shocking form of body art.

Modes of body modification used for centuries in other countries have just become popular in Western cultures. There are many places in the world where these art forms are not only the "fashion" but have been traditional customs for centuries.

Many people in African nations decorate their faces in the name of fashion. Many color or dye their entire bodies with simple materials, such as clay, mud, and ashes.

Women who live in the region of the Sahel in Northern Africa pierce their ears with thin, sharp thorns and wear silver or brass loop earrings. Their temples and cheeks are tattooed with geometric designs and the corners of their mouths with fan-shaped patterns. In the name of fashion, the men of some tribes shave their hairlines to accentuate their foreheads and, then, apply a powder to lighten the skin. These nomads wear elaborate headdress and jewelry. They use black kohl on the eyelids and lips and a line, usually white, to elongate the nose. Last of all, they draw white circles and dots on their faces. They excel at putting on make-up because their ceremonial appearances demand such a skill. At special festivals and dances, the women judge and select their mates on elegance and beauty.

For beauty, the Fulani women of Mali wear giant, hand-wrought, gold earrings suspended from ear lobe piercings. The jewelry is valued for its workmanship and is sometimes worth twenty head of cattle, or 3,000 American dollars. The women wear them as a display of wealth and status and, of course, fashion.

Another example of traditional fashion are the desert dwellers of North Africa who make intricate designs with henna on their hands and feet to focus attention as they dance. The Tuareg, another group of indigenous people, protect their faces with veils. Some veils are traditionally dyed blue by pounding indigo into the cloth. Much of the dye rubs off on the wearer. The effect has earned the Tuareg people the title, "blue men of the desert." The brass and aluminum for telephone and telegraph wires are used by the herdsmen of northern Kenya to make ornaments of earrings and aluminum lip and ear-flap plugs.

Media and Advertising

Another possible explanation for the popularity of body modification is the influence of the media and advertising.

Current themes for fashion advertising are individuality and nonconformity. The message of rebellion is subliminal. Advertisers push products by telling the viewer that their particular products will make them appear more unique, thus more valued. One extravagantly made commercial says: "You're not John Doe. Why drive his car?" The pictures which accompany the words are a montage of leather jackets, handsome boots, spike-heeled shoes, and beautiful women. A close-up of a tribal tattoo on a man's shoulder tells the viewer that body modification is acceptable and the fashionable thing to do.

Fashion Designers

Jean-Paul Gaultier started his career as a fashion designer at the age of eighteen as an assistant to well-known fashion designer Pierre Cardin. Gaultier is celebrated for designing the cone bra worn by Madonna on her 1990 Blonde Ambition Tour. He is also known for punk fashion and the costumes he has designed for successful stage plays. Recently, at a show in Paris, Gaultier presented a spectacular runway collection of clothing representing tattoos and piercing of African, Indian, European, and American influences. Tube dresses, sarongs, jackets, and leggings, which were printed on sheer, flesh-colored fabric, gave the illusion of naked skin. These garments were decorated with sun, hand, snake, motorcycle, and money motifs.

Included in the fashion show was a lavish display of face jewelry for piercings. This was featured with nose cuffs and studs, dangle earrings and hoops, and clusters of eyebrow jewels. The models also had temporary tattoos at their necklines and on their hands, wrists, arms and ankles. In addition, some of the models had ornate patterns for belly button tattoos. For the extravaganza, he used nonprofessional models, found at a tattoo convention in London, who were ideal for his work.

With his creations, Gaultier presented the startling vision of cross-cultural harmony of piercing and tattoos. "I wanted to point out the tribal roots of body art and offer a little history lesson," Gaultier is quoted as saying.

Recently, a picture spread of Gaultier's exotic garments appeared in a high fashion magazine. The career models shown, not only wore elegant clothing, but had stunning designs on their bodies and exquisite jewels on their faces. Other fashion designers have followed Gaultier's lead and produced collections that feature tattoo-parlor techniques on T-shirts, tights, and dresses.

In a recent magazine that features tattooing art, an article appeared under the title "Vintage Threads." It reports that years back, designer Betsey Johnson offered a line of clothing with flash designs by Mark Mahoney. With the short article are pictures of a tattooed model wearing a flesh colored top with the black designs of mermaids, tiger heads, stars, roses,checkered flags, and flowing banners.

Permanent Cosmetic Make-up

You may not realize that permanent make-up is actually a form of tattooing. Actors, models, singers, and other high profile people often get cosmetic tattooing for the convenience of not having to apply make-up every day.

Eyebrows, upper and lower eyelids, and lips are most commonly tattooed. Permanent eyeliner generally lasts longest, four to six years, before it begins to fade. Brows and lipliner need to be reapplied after two to four years. Cheek color can also be tattooed. Eyeshadow requires a specialty for shading, and undereye concealer is tricky to color in evenly. The technique of cosmetic tattooing is referred to as "permanent cosmetic make-up." For a lot of people, it is the most mainstream and least offensive form of tattooing.

Beauty salons in Korea employ cosmeticians who provide permanent make-up, along with facials, manicures, and bikini waxes. People who do this type of work live all over the globe, practicing in such places as Paris, Seoul, Los Angeles, and New York.

In many areas of the world, cosmetologists are encouraged to enroll in seminars to learn about permanent make-up and how to cover over old tattoos and scars. The learning process is comparable to that of a tattoo artist. People who apply permanent make-up generally don't refer to themselves as tattooists, instead, they regard themselves as skilled and well-trained artists who do cosmetic and reconstructive tattooing. Medical doctors who do cosmetic tattoos refer to it as surgery, or micropigment implantation.

Scar cover-up and nominal body reconstruction were done in America almost a century ago. Chuck Eldridge of the Tattoo Archive in Berkeley, California, says that East Coast society ladies began having lip and cheek color and eyeliner tattooed on themselves in the early 1920s.

Permanent make-up is also popular and fashionable for men as well as women. "People 18-35 and in the alternative music scene have permanent make-up because it's a time saver. One of my friends has tattooed sideburns and eyebrows. He looks great." Among the well-known entertainers who have had this performed are soul singer, James Brown, real-estate magnate, Donald Trump, former Miss America, Mary Ann Mobley, and pop singer, Michael Jackson.

Reconstructive Surgery

Tattoos can be applied to hide scars or to offer a solution to a surgical situation. After writer Deena Metzger had a breast removed because of cancer, she had a tree tattooed across the scar. In her book *Tree, Essays and Pieces*, she describes her feelings: "I am no longer afraid of mirrors. There is a fine red line across my chest where a knife entered, but now a branch winds about the scar and travels from arm to heart. Green leaves cover the branch, grapes hang there and a bird appears. I think the bird is singing. When he finished his work, the tattooist drank a glass of wine with me. I have relinquished some of the scars. I have designed my chest with the care given to an illuminated manuscript."

Sports Figures

Besides a portrait of his daughter, a Harley-Davidson motorcycle, a cross, and a shark, the contents of the Louvre appear to have been tattooed on Dennis Rodman's body. Rumor has it that Rodman has tattooing done in every city where he plays. "This is the reason some of his tattoos are bad, bad, bad," an artist contends. He doesn't have time to check out where the quality work is done."

Recently, on a television program, Rodman sat for a nose piercing. At first the orange, green, yellow, and blue haired basketball player was uncomfortable. After a moment, he allowed the piercing to proceed and had a large ring placed in his nostril. TV talk-show host, Larry King, asked him why he had piercings. His reply was that he wants to look good and he likes a little pain.

Chauncey Billups, NBA basketball player, has the word, "SMOOTH," tattooed on his biceps. "That's the way he plays, with smooth movements," the sportscaster says when he reports a televised game. Other famous sports figures who have tattoos are Mike Tyson, former heavyweight champion, and Shaquille "Shaq" O'Neal of the Los Angeles Lakers.

The familiar USA Olympic emblem of connected circles is a popular tattoo with Olympic champions, as well as, amateur high school and college athletes. Sportspeople at the 1997 Olympic games had artists in Atlanta tattoo the Olympic rings on their bodies. Swimmer, Amy Vandyken, has the traditional rings on her ankle, serving as a permanent reminder of her Olympic experience.

In the last few years, rock stars, movie stars, sports stars and superstar models have embraced skin art. Harrison Ford's favorite object is an earring in his left ear because, he says, "It looks neat." Mature and reserved *60 Minutes* interviewer, Ed Bradley, also wears an earring.

In *The Total Tattoo Book*, by Amy Krakow, some of the following celebrities are listed as having tattoos:

Whoopi Goldberg, LaToya Jackson, Cher, Ozzy Osbourne, Joan Baez, Julia Roberts, Jon Bon Jovi, Sean Connery, John Kennedy Jr., Drew Barrymore, Melanie Griffith, Tony Danza, Nicholas Cage, Johnny Depp, Mickey Rourke, and Charlie Sheen. One look at MTV will show a number of rock stars with multiple tattoos and piercings.

Celebrities and the rich and famous have always had a strong influence on fashion. Many teens are influenced by what their favorite rock stars or movie idols wear, say, and do. When the artist formerly known as Prince and his wife were seen with henna designs on their hands and feet, it became a trend for a short time. Fashion and entertainment magazines started showing other celebrities with similar designs. Gwen Stefani, lead singer of No Doubt, also had henna designs and is often seen wearing a bindi, an Indian form of decoration. It is important to know that to follow a particular interest or fashion is a choice and up to the individual.

But keep in mind that interests and fashions change. Even some celebrities regret their actions. Johnny Depp had a partial removal of a tattoo that read "Winona Forever" after his relationship with Winona Ryder ended, and Roseanne Barr had the tattooed name of her ex-husband, Tom Arnold, removed.

Alternatives to Tattooing and Piercing

Fashion has sometimes been used to protest what's going on in the world and to assert group membership. Hippies and flower children wore beads and tye-dyed clothing.

Punk rockers dressed in black and wore their hair in spiked and colored mohawks. For years outlaw bikers have worn leather jackets, boots, and oversized belt buckles. These styles were used at different times to symbolize dissatisfaction with mainstream values. Every young person wants to have a style and dress that's as fashionable as that of their peers. The big difference is that these current trends in body art are more or less permanent. There are ways to get around being indelibly marked, such as temporary tattoos and jewelry designed to look like piercing jewelry, and still make a statement.

Fake Tattoos

Early in the century, fake tattoos could be purchased ten for a penny in a candy store. Since the year 1912, stamp-sized tattoos have often been the treasured prize found in a five-cent box of Cracker Jack. Today, the cost of Cracker Jack has gone up, but the toy surprises remain the same: a whistle, a miniature flag, or a fake tattoo. All you have to do is place the tiny square on the back of a hand, press with a damp sponge, and a design appears.

Temporary tattoos can also be purchased in gift and craft stores. They can look very much like the real thing. The method is easy. The simple instructions may read: "Remove from protective sheet, press on skin, wet back with a sponge, wait thirty seconds, and peel off backing." Some tattoo packages include a special paint for coloring. This makes it possible for a person to judge which colors work best and look the most attractive. If the design is not what the person had in mind, he or she can wash it off and start all over. Outlining the tattoo with black ink can make the nonpermanent motif look more real.

Some tattoo shops offer sophisticated forms of body painting, including temporary tattoos. This work is done easily by using a transfer tattoo. The job is finished as soon as the transfer paper is peeled away. Other temporary tattoos are more complex, involving a black-stenciled outline which is painstakingly filled in with liquid paint on a tiny brush. This can take thirty minutes or more and can cost between twenty and forty dollars. You can also make do-it-yourself tattoos using washable-ink pens to adorn your body.

Imitation Piercing

In the movie *Fly Away Home* an observant viewer might catch a glimpse of the young heroine, played by Anna Paquin, wearing a nose cuff. In one scene, Anna's character, Amy, adjusts the nose jewelry with the help of a friend.

A fake nose ring or cuff is easy to make and comfortable to wear. With bead pliers, a person cuts off the friction post of a wide-band earring, and then folds the ornament and presses it onto either the broad part of the nostril or the nostril septum.

Stores that specialize in hair decorations, bangles, and unusual socks, often carry merchandise known as "faux piercing jewelry." These pieces do not require a piercing hole; the jewelry is pressed on. Sometimes, a magnet holds the ring, stud, or spike in place.

Fashion is a mirror, which reflects the ever-changing trends of our culture. Appearance and looks have always been a major part of our culture, but, unlike clothes and make-up, tattoos and piercing are a more committed form of fashion. While it is natural for teens to embrace the current fads, or even rebel against them, choosing a tattoo, piercing, or brand takes more consideration than buying this year's latest jeans or wearing the newest hair-style.

During the 1950s, the style was poodle skirts and saddle shoes. Adults were appalled by the long hair on men in the 1960s. Bell-bottom pants and wide-collar shirts were all the rage in the 1970s. Styles of those days were as much of an enigma to the previous generation as the fashion statement of a nose ring is to the previous generation today.

Those who study or work with teens say that each generation tries to do something the other has not done before. They conclude that the tattoo, piercing, and branding craze is a way for young people to separate themselves from the mainstream. "Whether these modes of body modification are fad or fashion in the Western world remains to be seen," says Dr. Kitty Knabbe. "It will depend on how long the appeal lasts. Right now, tattoos, piercings, and brandings are considered by the young to be a form of fashion," she says. "Unfortunately, it may also be the scarred and disfigured outcome for tomorrow's middle-aged."

Tattooing, piercing, and branding are very individual forms of expression. Before you decide to follow such a trend, think about the reasons why you might want to make such a permanent statement. If your reasons are based on the fact that everyone else is doing it, you may want to give it some more thought. It is always a good idea to give careful consideration to any big decision you make in your life, not just when it comes to body modification. Then, you can be sure the decision is right for you.

Making The
Right Decision

Brian is interested in eventually getting a tattoo. He has talked to a tattoo artist and knows that the design he wants will cost around $150. He has also checked out the studio where he hopes to go. "It's clean. The place is safe because the guy who does the work has disposable needles and uses steam cleaning for the other tools. He also uses new ink pots every time he gives a tattoo."

Brian has friends who are tattooed and says he knows girls who have stylish "tats" on their ankles and inner thighs. "Getting a tattoo is a radical act, but it's different now. Eventually, people from my generation will all have tattoos," he says. "Still, it's a monumental decision, and there are a lot of things to consider."

This young man is right when he says that there are a lot of things to consider. Let's look at those considerations.

Employment

Every year, there are hundreds of applications for employment at Disneyland in Anaheim, California. The pay is good, the environment is pleasant, and most of the jobs are just plain fun. However, this resort, like most vacation spots, has firm rules for the people that work there. The employers consider appearance a necessary part of their overall show. Applications note: "All cast members must comply with the official guidelines and have the 'Disney Look'."

To get a job at Disneyland, it is necessary for the women to have what is described as "the natural look." This means that only make-up of natural tones may be worn, simple hair styles are required, limited jewelry used, and no visible tattoos.

For men, Disney requires "a conservative look." This means hair cut above the ears, clean shaven, no more than one ring and one watch, and no visible tattoos.

Their employment policy may sound old-fashioned, but that's what people feel is so wonderful about Disneyland. That's why millions of people from all over the world visit every year. It is a reminder of a time when life was less complicated. Besides, when someone is hiring you and paying you, he or she has the right to enforce these guidelines.

A tattoo or a facial piercing is especially noticeable and distracting for anyone working in the food industry.

Robin works as a waitress in a first-class restaurant in Espanola, New Mexico. She has a pretty smile and wears multiple gold and silver earrings in both of her ear piercings. She does not have other body piercings, but she does have a tattoo on her hand between her thumb and forefinger joint. "Previously," she says, "it was a cross but was messed up in the application. The artist tried to cover it up with a picture of a blue rose." A flower and a banner with the word 'LaRaza' appears on her forearm. "Back then, it was unusual for a young girl to have tattoos," she explains. "I felt that it would show the pride that I have in being a Hispanic daughter. Because I am older and have grown into an independent woman, I no longer need to be reminded that I am my own person. Now, as a food server, I'd rather not have visible tattoos as it causes unnecessary attention. Tourists often ask what they mean, and why I have them. I never wish to appear rude, but on a busy day or during the rush hours, it takes time to explain.

Robin says she has been telling her daughter and her daughter's friends not to have tattoos. "I tell them when I did this ,it had a special meaning. Now, tattooing doesn't seem to be related to where a person lives, their race, age, a particular philosophy, or religion. I am also aware that tattoos can cause problems in the job place."

The Big Decision

When someone is considering a tattoo, piercing, or brand the first question that comes into his or her mind is: Who do I talk to about such a big decision? Chances are you have already discussed it with your best friend, a sibling, or a boyfriend or girlfriend. Maybe they like the idea and agree that you should have some body art. Perhaps, they are thinking about being tattooed, pierced or branded, also.

Your first step in whether or not to get a tattoo, piercing or branding is to talk it over with your parents. No one in your life cares more about you, and no one has a greater responsibility for your well-being. It is important what your parents think, even if you don't agree with them. They may even have tattoos, piercings, or brands, and their ideas on the subject will be helpful. They may approve wholeheartedly or they may object, depending on their taste and personal experiences. Whatever their opinion may be, you will want to listen. The results of monumental decisions can have lasting and long term results, good and bad, in families.

A favorite teacher or school counselor can be helpful if you are thinking about body art. The first thing most will tell you is that you must be eighteen before you can be tattooed or pierced, unless you have a parent's approval. If you are younger than the legal age, it gives you more time to give serious thought to such a monumental decision. They will probably say that what you want and need now will be totally different from what you want in your twenties and thirties. They will tell you that being "cool" as a young adult is not necessarily the same as being an interesting, attractive, or inspirational person later in life.

Peer Pressure

The enthusiasm for the body art of today might be compared with the vogue of cigarette smoking in an earlier era. For years, almost everyone smoked because it was the popular thing to do. It was something to talk about and share. It was something people did so they would have something to do with their hands. Famous people and movie stars were rarely seen without holding a cigarette as a trademark of their sophistication and glamour. Holding a cigarette, lighting it, and blowing smoke became an art form. Smoking was almost conventional. The advertisements were enticing. Peer pressure was so powerful that the young person who didn't smoke was often considered a prude, an outsider, and even strange.

Years later, people have learned that smoking is an addiction and a health hazard. While body art does not pose the same dangers of cigarettes, there are some similarities. Being tattooed, pierced, or branded is expensive and can cause serious health problems. A person can, and often does, become addicted. One tattoo, piercing, or branding is a rarity.

Body Art Addiction

It's difficult to explain exactly why body art can become addictive for some people. When you ask people what it feels like to get a tattoo, a piercing, or a brand, some may tell you that the procedure gives them a high and makes them feel powerful and confident. Some report that the pain of the procedure releases endorphins (the body's natural painkillers). This feeling can be the motivation behind more and more body art—to achieve that feeling of empowerment again. But some people make quick decisions, based on those feelings, and get more (or bigger) tattoos or piercings, which they may regret at a later time.

"I felt so good after my first tattoo—like I could do anything—that I decided to get another one as soon as possible. Since the first one was small and not very visible, I thought I should get something bigger,

92

where everyone could see it. I felt very proud of the fact that I was strong and brave enough to get a tattoo. But a few years later, I began to regret the second one. I wish I had put more thought into it."

It may be difficult to resist today's rage to get tattooed, pierced, or branded. While many people indulge in body art to set themselves apart from others, the growing popularity of tattooing, piercing, and branding has made these practices a part of popular culture. It's as if *not* having any body art is what will set you apart as an individual.

After years of thinking about it, Terry, a Vietnam veteran, finally decided to get a tattoo. "Lots of guys had tattoos done when they were in the war," he says. "They cost next to nothing. The lonesome soldier needed something that made him feel good about himself. Something permanent, say a girlfriend's or a buddy's name, or a unit's number tattooed on his body, did that.

"Often, when a guy was on R and R, say in Bangkok, he'd get a tattoo that didn't mean anything because he was probably drunk or on drugs. It was something to do to get away from the boredom. I didn't have the need to get a tattoo, although I thought about it. Mostly, I thought about my family and wanted to get home alive.

"Years later, I was still thinking about a tattoo. It's an idea that has always fascinated me. Part of my problem has been that I wasn't sure what I wanted permanently struck on my body. Another consideration was what my children would say. We're a fairly

conservative family, and I appreciate my wife's and children's opinions. We usually consult one another about issues that could affect one another. Having a tattoo was too much of an issue not to get input from Marianne, Corey, Evan, and Alexandra.

"Years ago, an Arapaho Indian friend did a water-color of an eagle's head as a gift for me. I've always enjoyed this piece of art. I decided that if I were to have a tattoo, it would be a replica of that particular portrait. After a family meeting, where I assumed that everyone was in agreement about this choice, I had an artist tattoo a replica the eagle's head on my right bicep." Terry's tattoo is truly beautiful. The picture on Terry's biceps looks more like a watercolor than a tattoo. "When I show it to anyone they are impressed and make comments like, 'Wow,' 'It's stunning,' and 'You made the perfect choice,' he says."

Terry's story is unusual because of the fact that he thought long and hard before he got his tattoo. He consulted family members to see how they felt about his decision.

Certainly, there are a lot of motives for getting a tattoo, but the most common reasons seem to be the need for personal identity and the desire for attention. Neither idea is wrong. A young person may believe life will somehow magically change if he or she does something "different."

Being in Love

Gracia has large, dark eyes and black hair that swings down to her waist. When she was seventeen, she met Stephen who is an artist. She was pleased

94

when Stephen opened a tattoo shop in the small California town where she lived and even more pleased, when he asked her to work as a receptionist and bookkeeper. The pair was together in the shop all day, six days a week. When there were no customers, Stephen taught Gracia to do piercing. In exchange for these lessons, Gracia allowed Stephen to tattoo some of his designs on her legs and arms. Gracia realized that her mom and dad would object, but she knew the designs could be easily hidden with long sleeves and jeans. Having Stephen tattoo her, put his art on her body, seemed the right thing to do because she loved him so much and he had, many times, told her of his love. Stephen suggested a tattoo of a snake, starting from the nape of her neck, across her shoulders and down to the small of her back. She readily agreed.

Stephen outlined a picture on her back of a cobra with a spread hood, menacing eyes, and big fangs. Often, as the artist did his work, customers dropped into the studio and were invited to watch. It was a lot of pain for Gracia, but knowing how proud Stephen was of his work and her beautiful skin, she did not protest. After weeks of work, the tattooed outline was ready for color.

At this point, Stephen and Gracia had a terrible fight. Stephen physically abused Gracia, and she ended up in the hospital with a broken arm. Stephen went to jail and was charged with battery. Gracia's parents discovered that their underage daughter was covered with tattoos and filed a lawsuit.

Gracia is now recovering from a broken arm and a broken heart. Every time she takes a shower, dresses, or looks into a mirror, she sees the tattoos and thinks about Stephen. She thinks about the good times but about the terrible times, too. She knows that the tattoos will always remind her of Stephen. She worries about the cost of having "Stephen's markings" removed and if she will ever be able to afford laser surgery. Right now, that is all she can think of. She wants the tattoos removed so that she can get on with her life.

The story of Gracia and Stephen may seem outrageous, yet it is true, and there are more like it. Most people don't have numerous tattoos put on their bodies as Gracia did in order to prove her love for Stephen, but many do have a name or special design tattooed on their body as a reminder of a special person and a special affection. Later, they spend a lot of time and money trying to get it removed.

Frequently, people change their minds about the romance in their lives, relationships falter, love affairs fail, and marriages dissolve. Being in love with Cheri and having "Janet" tattooed on a forearm can and will cause big-time problems. It could be embarrassing to have, Ron, tattooed on a shoulder and become engaged to Kyle. Having a crush is not the best reason for getting a tattoo. Some very good advice is given by a professional tattooer of many years: "Never have a living person's name, initials, or portrait tattooed on your body." An exception may be tattoos that honor parents or relatives as these relationships often don't change the way lovers do.

Religious Considerations

Tattooing has had different meanings that have changed

over the generations. Sometimes, tattoos have been marks of compassion, devotion, and inner strength. In other periods, tattooing has had a sinister history.

The Holocaust

During World War II, Jews were rounded up, put in cattle cars, and shipped to concentration camps. For most, it was a death sentence by hunger, cold, medical experimentation, gas, or ovens. For those who survived, it was and remains a nightmare. Besides the horror, many inhumane acts were thrust daily upon the people. Among these was the tattooing of all prisoners with six little numbers for identification. This presented an unspeakable ordeal because, according to Jewish law, being tattooed means he or she can never be buried in a Jewish cemetery.

In his book *The Drowned and the Saved*, Primo Levi writes: "The [tattoo] operation was not very painful and lasted no more than a minute, but it was traumatic. Its symbolic meaning was clear to everyone: this is an indelible mark, you will never leave here; this is the mark with which slaves are branded and cattle sent to slaughter, and this is what you have become. You no longer have a name; this is your new name." Primo Levi's number was 174517.

He goes on to say that, "At a distance of years, my tattoo has become a part of my body. I don't glory in it, but I am not ashamed of it either; I do not display and do not hide it. I show it unwillingly to those who ask out of pure curiosity; readily and with anger to those who say they are incredulous [doubtful]. Often young people ask me why I don't have it erased, and this surprises me: Why should I? There are not many of us in the world to bear this witness."

Jewish or not, many people decide not to indulge in body art because of religious beliefs. Religion is an important and personal part of many people's lives. It is certainly a reason to seriously consider whether or not to be tattooed, pierced, or branded.

Real Experiences

Many people have wonderful stories of how and why they became involved in body art, while some have had unfortunate experiences to relate. Renee, a tattoo artist, tells a charming story about an experience and a follow-up story about a client.

"Some years ago, I tattooed brightly colored, geometric designs on the belly of a woman who was two months pregnant. On a few occasions, the woman came into the shop and showed me the tattoo. As her pregnancy progressed, the tattoo blew up like writing on the side of a balloon. This mommy has since told me that she thinks it was a good idea to have the tattoos done while she was pregnant. Her son, now five years old, loves his mother's tattoos. He is sweet tempered and unusually artistic. His mother attributes much of Caleb's personality and creativity to tattoo."

Not all stories are as delightful as Renee's. Bob, all muscles and black leather, wanted a tattoo of a scorpion on the outside of his calf. He assumed it would hurt some, but he never thought he would pass out. "I wasn't in pain, but every time I thought about the needles in my skin, everything ceased. I blanked out right there in the chair. The first two times, the artist was concerned and awakened me. The third time, she just kept tattooing away." Bob felt embarrassed and decided not to have his tattoo finished. Today, he lives with an outline of a scorpion on his leg to remind him he is not as tough as he thought he was.

A National Survey

USA Weekend is a newspaper insert that reaches 41.7 million readers every Sunday. In May of 1997, a national survey was published in which 218,350 students spoke out on teens and their freedom. Some of the issues reviewed were safety, health, school rules, values, race, parents, drugs and alcohol. The study also included the question: "When Can Teens Get a Tattoo or Nose Ring?" Twenty percent of the respondents thought body piercing, other than ears, should be okay at age sixteen. Seventeen percent thought it should be all right to get a tattoo at age seventeen. A timely and mature discussion with seven teenagers ensued. Their lively remarks were as follows:

> Jabari: "At my age, you often make silly decisions about what you want and don't want. Say you want a tattoo today—you may not want it tomorrow."

> Kimberly: "It's just an immature act by adolescents, who do things impulsively."

> Miyun: "At our age, we can't really afford tattoos.

Body piercing right now is No.1. Ears are fine—but all over your face? That's a little much."

Helen: "That's just because we're not used to seeing it on places like the belly button. I don't think we should say where is the right place."

Jaime: "A boy in my class had piercings all over his face, and it was distracting."

Gore: "I think I'll spend more time talking to my son. (laughter) It is a bit extreme, self-mutilation of the face. Should there be an age limit?"

Amy: "I think eighteen for everything."

Jabari: "But if there's a law, teens will find an unsafe way to do it."

A Piercer's Opinion

R.G. is a professional piercer. She works by appointment only and often makes house calls. "Sometimes, people in their early teens want a piercing," she says. "The problem here is that kids don't realize how much attention it takes. Sure, mentally a youngster can care for it, but the physical body keeps growing. The mind keeps growing, too. The truth is that people don't know who they are until their mid-twenties.

"If they have a rock 'n' roll tattoo, the love for it may pass. Young people live in the moment. It's hard to explain to young people that everything passes, and you change. It is better to wait for these things until you have a wider view of life."

Most people agree that any kind of body art requires serious thought. Ray, a Native American who considers English to be his second language, would agree wholeheartedly and says that many Native Americans have piercings. His ear lobe punctures were done as a family tradition when he was a small child. Ray's tattoo of an eagle and chest plate with a peace pipe was done as a religious ceremony when he was in his early teenage years. "Body decorations should be done only with serious consideration. They should have meaning and be performed under dignified circumstances," he says.

Opinions Are Everywhere

Most people seem to have an opinion about body art. Everyone appears to have a thought, an idea, or a reason why he or she gets tattooed, pierced, or branded. People approve with excitement in their voices and pride in their eyes or disapprove with a shrug of the shoulders and turned-down mouths. Read what these people have to say about the subject. You'll find that opinions and experiences vary as much as the people themselves.

John, age 10: My parents told me if my grades were good this year, I could have an ear piercing. My grades were good. I went and had my ear pierced. It sort of stung when I had it done. It really looks good.

Gretchen, age 15: When I went to Water World last weekend I saw that at least half the people there had tattoos and piercings. It looked okay, but I'd never do it because I couldn't take the pain.

Joshua, age 16: Right now, I'm going to a Christian school. The school doesn't allow us to wear jewelry, and if anyone has a tattoo, it's covered. As soon as I'm of legal age, I'll have a Latin phrase, *Carpe Diem*, which means Seize the Day, tattooed on my right shoulder. I have no idea about the cost, but I'll go to a professional artist.

Bronwyn, age 18: I have an ankh on the back of my neck. The tattoo is my jewelry, and I get a lot of compliments. I realize that when I get older I may not want the tattoo. For a simple solution, I'll let my hair grow long.

Vinnie, age 19: When I get a tattoo, I consider it an act of rubbing culture into my body. My tattoos are my second skin, and that's where I'm the most comfortable.

Rose, age 20: My boyfriend tattooed a rose between my thumb and forefinger which has now faded into a dark-looking cloud. I was young, stupid I guess. Someday, I hope to have it removed.

Craig, age 21: My job is working at a fast-food mart. I have eight piercings, five of them on my face plus a tongue bolt. When I first started working here, the management said the "look" could be harmful to customer service. Actually, over time, shoppers seem to have accepted my looks.

Clive, age 24: When people see my tattoos they always ask the same questions. "Are your tattoos real?" "Did it hurt?" "Are you glad you got tattooed?" The answers are "Yes," "Yes," and "Yes."

Candace, age 25: When I was in junior high a lot of girls tattooed each other with a darning needle and a pencil eraser. We didn't think about germs or infections. We were trying to impress the guys in school that we were nonconformist. When I became an adult, I had a professional artist redo the mess I had made ten years earlier.

Bill, age 46: When I grew up only sailors and prisoners had tattoos. I didn't want to worry that I might not want it later. I haven't changed my mind since I was a kid. They're ugly. I don't want my children to have a tattoo, but it's up to them.

Mr. Kirkwood, age 56: If I had time, I'd go to high schools and show the kids what tattoo removal looks like. I'd tell them that it hurts like hell to have these things scraped or burned off. I'd tell them that being tattooed could be a big mistake, and they'd better think long and hard before they get involved.

The Bottom Line

Some people consider the art of tattoo to be traditional American folk art and a major cultural expression. Certainly there's a story behind every tattoo, piercing, and branding. Melinda teaches special education at an elementary school. She often wears a pin with rainbow colors that signifies gay pride. She has a tattoo above her left breast with riding waves of rainbow colors. She says, "I like my tattoo, but I gave the venture a lot of thought before I had it done." Whatever the situation, it's important to think about the pros and cons before having your body permanently marked, pierced, or burned.

Starlet and Jesse are seventeen and in love. As soon as they reach the legal age of eighteen they are planning to have identical designs tattooed on their biceps. One tattooist suggested that Starlet and Jesse should reconsider having their names tattooed on each other's arm. Jesse told the tattooist that if he and Starlet broke up, he would have her name removed with laser. "The guy got real mad," Jesse says. "He told me a person shouldn't think about getting a tattoo removed before he gets one. He said that's like going to a divorce lawyer before you get married."

This tattooist gave excellent advice. Karol, another tattoo artist, recommends: "No matter what kind of a tattoo you get with another person in celebration of a relationship, the image will remind you of your partner. However, if the relationship ends, you'll be much happier with a simpler tattoo that strikes a chord in your heart rather than with one that says 'Bobby Forever,' especially if Bobby is gone. Future loves can be hurt by the tattoo of another person's name on your body. Often, the tattooed person will feel the need to get another name tattoo to ease the new lover's feelings. In my opinion, you shouldn't get tattoos for anyone else. It's not about what other people mean to you: it's about what you mean to yourself."

Getting Rid of
Unwanted Body Art

One big question that comes to mind when people discuss tattooing, piercing, and branding is: What happens if you are unhappy with the decision and want to get rid of your tattoos, piercings, or branding?

Hopefully, if you've followed the advice offered here, you'll never find yourself in this situation. But what do you do if your tattoo, piercing, or brand turns out badly? For example, the tattooist talked you into something you don't like. You knew it was all wrong when you agreed to the design but were too embarrassed to protest. Now, you're sorry that you ever got involved. You can't show it to your friends because if they laugh you would feel humiliated. Your parents will get angry, your brother or sister will say you spent a lot of money for nothing, and your skin is so sore and tender you want to cry out loud.

First, visit body art studios, interview the artists, and find someone whom you feel you can trust. Frankly discuss your problem with him or her. Most likely, this person will be understanding and help you with a solution. The remedy may be something simple, like having a different design placed over an unattractive one, or the artist may recommend that you have the objectionable tattoo, piercing, or branding removed with laser.

Some Reasons for Having Body Art Removed

↪ Regret after getting body art on spur of the moment.

↪ Tattoo placement interferes with getting a job.

↪ A romance has ended.

↪ Poor workmanship.

↪ Tattoo is gang-related.

↪ Change in lifestyle.

↪ Allergic reaction.

Regret

Tattooing and piercing establishments frequently cater to "drop-in" customers. It isn't always necessary to make an appointment. If the artist is not busy, he or she is often free to work on a client. Many people get a tattoo or piercing on the spur-of-the-moment. When asked why, many men and women answered, "Don't know."

Spontaneity can lead to regret after getting any type of body art on a whim. Many people, who make hasty decisions about permanent body modification, are eventually sorry about some aspect of their decision. Perhaps, it is the choice of a design, the placement of the art, or the selection of the artist.

Getting a Job

Tattoos are often a hindrance to educational and employment opportunities. It is not always easy for a person to rid themselves of a tattoo, especially if it appears in plain sight, such as on the face, neck, wrists, fingers, knuckles, or palms. Most removal techniques leave scars, and those that don't are very expensive. It's sometimes difficult to think far into your future and make decisions based on what might be. But getting a job or getting into college often depends on someone else's opinion, and you have no way of knowing what kind of judgments that person will make about you.

Romance Ends

How you feel about your boyfriend or girlfriend now may not last for the rest of your life. People tend to have several relationships over the course of their lives and fall in love more than once. Getting a tattoo or a brand in honor of that relationship isn't always the best way to express strong feelings. Breaking up with someone is a difficult and painful experience. Trying to remove a tattoo or a brand will only provide more heartache in the end.

Bad Workmanship

Like everything else in life---excellent physicians versus bad physicians, good teachers versus bad teachers, fine speakers versus bad speakers---there are good and bad tattoo, piercing, and branding artists. Bad tattoo artists are still referred to as"scratchers," "jaggers," and "hackers." A tattoo with irregular lines, blurred designs, and faded colors is a reason some people decide to remove it. Bad placement or bad results are also reasons to remove piercings and brands.

Gang-Related

Secret hand signals, designated colors, and specific pieces of clothing have meaning and connect members of gangs. Tattooing, piercing, or branding are routine rituals held for new members. It is easy for a participant hoping to escape association with gangs to ignore hand signals, disregard specific colors, and omit wearing required clothing. It may not be difficult for a person to rid himself or herself of piercings. He or she has only to remove his or her jewelry, and, hopefully, the holes will grow together. Tattoos and brands, however, are typically harder to remove and may still mark a person as part of a gang when he or she is trying to leave that life in the past.

Change in Lifestyle

As with outdated music, clothes, and hairstyles, a person may become bored with his or her tattoos, piercings, or brandings. A person may also change the way they think or live. Many young people experiment with different attitudes and lifestyles. As people grow older, their philosophies change, and some become more conservative in their choices. It's important to remember that you may not always think the same way you do now about how you want to live your life.

Allergic Reactions

Thousands of tattoos are applied each year. A small percentage lead to an allergic reaction. This may be due to the red inks used in coloring the design. Other side effects have been reported, such as infection, abnormal swelling, and excessive itching. Serious problems such as hepatitis and syphilis, have been documented. If you have sensitive skin or any type of allergy, it's essential to speak to a doctor before getting any body art. It may be best not take the risk at all.

In the United States, tattoo pigments are loosely regulated by the Food and Drug Administration (FDA). The shades and lot numbers of pigments used on clients are generally not recorded, nor is the manufacturer of the product noted. If the patron has a skin reaction or decides to have a tattoo removed, lack of this knowledge could cause problems.

Most tattoo patrons are unaware that colors used for tattooing are not ink or paint materials in the general sense. Inks are often a combination of powders or compounds that contain blends of carbon and wood. Different ink, also may contain metal that combines iron, copper, and aluminum. If you are considering getting a tattoo, it's a good idea to make note of the pigments being used.

Laser Technology

Many people decide later in life that they no longer want their body art. Removal can be a complicated issue. With piercings, the healing process is relatively simple if rules of cleanliness are followed and proper care is given. Getting rid of a brand or a tattoo, however, is more difficult. Usually, they are removed with laser technology.

The technical definition of laser is light amplification by stimulated emission of radiation. Laser amplifies or magnifies radiation frequencies, or levels, within or near the range of visible light. For "erasing" tattoos, different colors of laser light are used to remove the ink. The laser light is selectively absorbed by the tattoo pigment. This breaks up the ink into small fragments. These fragments are absorbed by the body's immune system. The surrounding skin should not be disturbed. As a patient, you should ask your doctor about this, because laser, the light process that destroys whatever it touches, is not entirely without risks. Some lasers will erase a particular color sequence. Other lasers remove everything and actually can cause the skin to boil.

The use of the q-switched ruby, the q-switched alexanderite, and the q-switched nd:yag lasers have been proven effective in the removal of professional and nonprofessional tattoos.

For successful therapy, three to ten sessions usually are required. To completely remove a tattoo, appointments are spaced four to six weeks apart. Black and blue tattoos are the easiest to remove; green and yellow are the hardest. Even with modern equipment, superior knowledge, and professional assistance there are some tattoos that won't come off completely. It also depends on the types of inks that were used and how deeply they are embedded in the skin. Laser treatments are painful. Some who've experienced it say it's worse than getting the tattoo.

Some doctors offer an anesthetic to help ease any discomfort. The laser breaks up the skin, leaving it raw and sensitive. There will be bleeding. Doctors recommend taking aspirin or ibuprofen thirty minutes before the treatment to help with the pain as well. Taking care of the skin after each treatment is very important. The doctor will give you complete instructions. It's recommended that the skin be kept clean and moisturized. The skin will be sore, and it can take up to a month for it to heal and be ready for another treatment.

Other Methods of Tattoo Removal

Dermatologists are doctors who specialize in treating skin, hair, and nail problems. Plastic surgeons are also experts in treating skin problems. These professionals know that there are different types and depths of tattoos. He or she may recommend that the simplest and least expensive thing for removal would be to snip out the tattoo and sew the skin back together. Hand tattoos are difficult to remove, and a surgical method might be desirable. Skin from the thighs or buttocks is used to replace the thin, pliable covering of the back of the hand. This technique is called "excision," which means to cut away. Even with surgery, faint traces of the tattoo will remain. Hair growth will be disrupted. Last of all, because the melanin color-layer will be removed, the skin won't tan.

Dermabrasion, a method to remove acne scars, is also used to dispose of tattoos by scraping the unwanted area or spot.

Salabrasion, a process of rubbing the surface of the skin with salt, is also a procedure. Chemical peels are sometimes effective. These methods may leave scarring.

You may need to consider an orthodontist if the tattoo or brand is near your mouth, an opthamologist if the work is near your eyes, or an ear, eye, and nose specialist if the tattoo, or branding is close to your ears. Most of these professionals have an expertise in the use of laser equipment.

A successful attorney has a unique story about his tattoo removal, which took place before laser technology.

Mr. Kirkwood remembers being told that years ago, his uncle was tattooed at a carnival. The next day the uncle's arms were red and swollen with serious infection. The recovery period was long and painful. When he was young, Mr. Kirkwood was often cautioned by his father never to be tattooed, but he was fascinated with tattoos. His journey with tattooing began when he was sixteen or seventeen years old. His first tattoo was an eagle on his shoulder, and, eventually, he had tattoos on his arms, back, and legs.

When he decided that he wanted a tattoo on his chest, the artist ran the tattoo gun over Kirkwood's chest bone so he could get the feel of the needle. "It hurt and, for once, I didn't go through with it," he says.

In only a few years, Mr. Kirkwood decided that he had made a mistake and wanted the designs removed. By then, he was in the military. He talked with a plastic surgeon and argued that, because people often stared at him and made him feel uncomfortable, it could qualify for the Air Force's requirement of "psychological harm," which permitted cosmetic surgery. The doctor agreed to remove the tattoos.

Kirkwood had several of his large tattoos removed with a Brown Dermatone, which is a machine that looks like a wood plane with the blades vibrating very quickly. With this device, the surgeon cut off the tattoo at a depth of 1/50,000th of an inch. After a few hours, the bleeding stopped. A piece of healthy skin was removed from his thigh. It was applied to the raw area, pressure packed, and bandaged. For three days, Kirkwood remained immobile to insure that the healthy skin didn't die from body movement. When the bandage was removed, the area was black. It looked gruesome. Kirkwood was discouraged, but he was told the area would have been gray if it had not taken.

To increase blood circulation, the patient was lowered by harness into a whirlpool. When the bandages were finally removed, the cells of the healing skin had grown into the gauze bandage. It had to be eased off the raw nerve endings. "The pain of removing the bandage was the worst part of the process," he says. Each day, he was harnessed and lowered into a whirlpool for therapy. Over a period of nine months, he had six arm and back tattoos removed by this method. All of the skin grafting left scars.

Two decades have passed, and Mr. Kirkwood is working with a plastic surgeon and having laser work done to remove his remaining tattoos.

Adverse Information

There is a great deal of misinformation about body art. Friends, meaning to be helpful, may not know what they're talking about when giving advice about getting tattooed, pierced, or branded. Books, movies, and videos seem to glide over the pain of the process and, more often than not, send the wrong messages.

A mentally disordered character, played by Bruce Dern in the movie, *Tattoo*, kidnaps and then tattoos Maud Adams, an actress playing the part of a beautiful and successful model. The disturbed tattooist is never shown wearing hygienic gloves, and blood does not appear as he makes his designs. The heroine never appears to scab or to be in pain.

In *Teresa's Tattoo*, the main character appears with a large tattoo after a night of partying. When she wakes up the next morning, her reaction is one of mild surprise. These movies are, of course, unrealistic. They send messages that a tattoo is not painful, there is no blood, and the persons receiving it aren't concerned and uncomfortable.

Currently, tattoos have lost much of their stigma, and body piercing and branding seem to have created significant interest and appear to be acceptable. Many teens are captivated by the idea of using their bodies as an art canvas. The rich and famous are fascinated. So are teachers, lawyers, and doctors. Suddenly, body art has become "mainstream."

On the other hand, fashions and fads in America are short-lived and easily forgotten. If this is the case, multitudes of people, possibly including you, will want their body art removed, and dermatology and plastic surgery skills will be in great demand. One medical assistant reports that she receives five to ten requests each week for tattoo removal.

If you are seriously thinking about having your tattoos or brandings removed, you'll need to know which kind of doctor will meet your particular needs, how much time the process will take, and how much money it's going to cost. With this in mind, you may want to observe some simple steps in order to make choices.

➼ Discuss your situation with a close family member or dependable friend.

➼ Contact the artist that did your tattoo and find out which types of pigment he or she used.

➼ Get recommendations from people who have had successful experiences with having their body art removed.

➼ Decide if you need a plastic surgeon, dermatologist, or another type of medical doctor to do your body art removal.

➼ Make an appointment with the doctor to thoroughly discuss your surgery and expectations of the results.

➼ Find out about the surgery and healing procedures and the time involved.

➼ Check to see if your doctor has had experience doing tattoo, piercing, and branding removal.

➼ Inquire about the professional organizations to which the doctor belongs. Get the exact names and telephone numbers to find out about the requirements for belonging to that particular organization.

➼ Frankly discuss fees and financing with the doctor. Health insurance does not, as a rule, cover the cost of this type of care.

➼ Make your decision and call for an appointment.

A Final Word

Even though it's possible to remove a tattoo, a brand, or even get rid of a piercing, it is still very important to think long and hard about these decisions. Because body art, by its very nature, is permanent, the removal factor should not play a role in your decision. In other words, if you're thinking, "I can always get it removed if I don't like it later on," you might want to rethink your decision. Body art is a commitment that needs to be taken seriously, and is taken seriously by many of its artists and practitioners.

Remember that you don't need to rush into anything, even if you really want a tattoo, or all your friends already have one. You have a lot of time to think about it. Give yourself six months or even a year to be sure it's what you really want. Then, if you haven't changed your mind, you can be assured that you were smart and considerate about getting your body art. You can know that it really means something to you and represents a part of who you are. Or you may decide that it was just a passing phase and, now, you're not so sure about what you want to do. In that case, you'll be very glad you waited.

Making smart decisions is an essential part of everyone's life. As you grow older, you'll begin to see how much a person can change over time. No one can prove this to you—it's something you can only experience yourself. And no one can tell you whether or not you'll regret anything you do. Only you will know if the decisions you make today are the right ones for you in the future.

Glossary

AIDS acquired immune deficiency syndrome; a severe disease spread through body fluids such as semen and blood

autoclave a machine that sterilizes equipment with pressurized steam

biker a man or woman who belongs to a motorcycle gang and follows an alternative lifestyle that often involves tattoos

body piercing a procedure in which a sharp instrument is passed through a fold of skin or part of the body, often for the purpose of inserting jewelry

branding a procedure in which the skin is seared with a hot iron to produce a raised design

cover-up tattoo tattoo done to hide scars or the effects of surgery

dermabrasion a treatment in which the skin is scraped in order to remove unwanted tattoos or acne scars

dermatitis an inflammation of the skin which can be caused by piercing jewelry

dermatology the branch of medicine concerned with the skin, hair, and nails

excision in medicine, a surgical procedure in which skin is cut away; used for the removal of unwanted tattoos on the back of the hand

faux piercing jewelry jewelry that looks like regular piercing jewelry but can be worn by anyone

flash designs for tattoos

full custom work freehand tattoo design

henna a natural dye used to decorate the body in Africa and India

HIV human immunodeficiency virus; a retrovirus spread through body fluids and that causes AIDS

hygiene in body art, conditions and practices that protect the client from infection and disease

"jailhouse" tattooing ("joint style" tattooing) a style of tattooing done with simple materials by prisoners

"kiss of fire" ("slash and burn") a popular term for branding

laser technology a method for converting electromagnetic radiation to frequencies within or near the range of visible light; used to remove unwanted tattoos

micropigment implantation medical term for cosmetic tattooing

Moko the style of tattooing practiced by the Maori people of New Zealand

permanent cosmetic make-up cosmetic tattoos, including eyeliner, eye shadow, and cheek color, done by a specially trained artist

rite of passage a ceremony marking a person's transition from one stage of life to another

salabrasion a method of removing unwanted tattoos in which the skin is rubbed with salt

scratcher an untrained or bad tattooist

"slash and burn" ("kiss of fire") a popular term for branding

sterilization in tattoo and piercing studios, the process that removes live bacteria and other microorganisms from equipment

tattooing a procedure of permanently marking the skin with ink or dye

transfer tattoo a piece of paper imprinted with a design that is used to make a temporary tattoo

waiver (release form) a document signed by a client that protects a tattoo or piercing studio in case of a lawsuit

Where to Go for Help

Alliance of Professional Tattooists
7477 Baltimore-Annapolis Boulevard
Suite 205
Glen Burnie, MD 21061
(410) 768-1963

Association of Professional Piercers
519 Castro Street
Box 120
San Francisco, CA 94114

Contact your state health department to find out more about the laws and safety regulations for tattooing, body piercing, and branding. Look in the White Pages under Health.

If you decide that you want your tattoos, piercings, or brandings removed, it is important to seek medical help. Contact:

American Board of Medical Specialities
1007 Church Street, Suite 404
Evanston, IL 60201-5913
Web site: http://www.healthy.net/pan/cso/cioi/abms.htm

For a free list of five U.S. Board Certified Plastic Surgeons who perform laser treatment in your area contact:

American Board of Dermatology
(313) 874-1088

American Board of Cosmetic Surgery
(206) 775-3561

The American Board of Plastic Surgery
Seven Penn Center
1635 Market Street
Suite 400
Philadelphia, PA 19103-2204
(215) 587-9322

American Society for Dermatologic Surgery (ASDS)
930 North Meacham
Shaumberg, IL 60173
(800) 441-2737

The American Society of Plastic and Reconstructive Surgeons
(800) 635-0635

For Further Reading

Fraser, Kennedy. *The Fashionable Mind: Reflections on Fashion.* Boston: Godine, 1985.

Govenar, Alan. *American Tattoo: As Ancient as Time, As Modern As Tomorrow.* San Francisco: Chronicle Books, 1997.

Howe, Neil. and William Strauss. *"The New Generation Gap,"* The Atlantic Monthly, December, 1992. pp 67-89.

Kaplan, Leslie S. *Coping with Peer Pressure.* New York: The Rosen Publishing Group, Inc. Rev. ed. 1996.

Krakow, Amy. *The Total Tattoo Book.* New York: Warner Books, 1994.

Steward, Samuel M. *Bad Boys and Tough Tattoos.* New York: Harrington Hawthorn Press, 1990.

Stine, Megan. *Tattoo Mania: The Newest Craze in Wearable Art.* New York: Bantam, 1993.

Tucker, Marcia. *"Psst! Wanna See My Tattoo. . . ."* Ms. Magazine, April, 1996, p 29-33.

Vale, V. and Andrea Juno. Re/Search #12: Modern Primitives. Eugene, Oregon: Re/Search Publications, 1989.

Wirths, Claudine. *Choosing is Confusing: How to Make Good Choices, Not Bad Guesses.* Palo Alto, CA: CPP Books, 1994.

Index

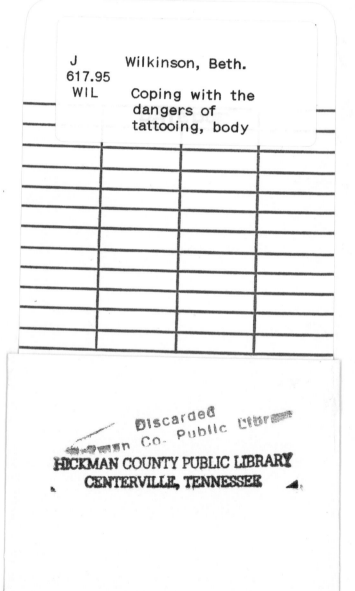